Mastering Soccer

Mastering Soccer

Lowell Miller

Contemporary Books, Inc.
Chicago

Library of Congress Cataloging in Publication Data

Miller, Lowell.
    Mastering soccer.

    Bibliography: p.
    Includes index.
    1. Soccer.   I. Title.
GV943.M554   796.33'42   78-31379
ISBN 0-8092-7324-1
ISBN 0-8092-7323-3 pbk.

All photos in this book, except where otherwise credited, are official North American Soccer League game photographs shot by George Tiedemann.

Published by Contemporary Books, Inc.
180 North Michigan Avenue, Chicago, Illinois 60601
Manufactured in the United States of America
Library of Congress Catalog Card Number: 78-31379
International Standard Book Number: 0-8092-7324-1 (cloth)
                             0-8092-7323-3 (paper)

Published simultaneously in Canada by
Beaverbooks
953 Dillingham Road
Pickering, Ontario L1W 1Z7
Canada

Contents

A Note to Women Players and Fans

Throughout this book you will find that team members are called "teammate" or "player" but are also referred to by means of masculine pronouns. We wish that there were some other way to handle the problem, but the English language just doesn't seem to have kept pace with the changes in society or in soccer. We were simply unable to come up with an alternative way of saying things that sounded right—passing to "him/her" or passing by "he or she" somehow seemed lacking in flow. So we felt compelled to settle for the traditional modes of expression. When you see a soccer player referred to as "him," please read it for yourself as "her" and accept our apologies.

1
Introduction

In most of the world, soccer is virtually a national obsession. The game as we know it is less than 150 years old, yet it's become no less an international, intercultural phenomenon than music or painting or friendship. Every country has its language, its customs, its myths, its uniqueness. Still, all over the globe a single sport reigns king. Soccer.

Only in the last decade has soccer become widely appreciated in the United States. It used to be a sport mainly for the Ivy League colleges and groups of immigrants. But that's been changing rapidly. In 1972 North American Soccer League attendance was a scant 400,000. By 1977 that figure had reached 3,500,000, with many teams playing to sellout crowds. On the amateur level, participation has risen 1,000 percent since 1965.

Soccer's catching on here, as it has caught on everywhere. There must be something special about the sport, some special energy that gets under the skin and flows around in the blood. But what is it?

On the field your light shoes are really your only piece of equipment. The wind blows through your shirt and around your legs as you run. You're constantly moving and constantly alert. You follow the bouncing ball. What will you do if it goes there, or there, or there? There's an open space. You run into it, creating an outlet for a pass. Then the space closes again. You look for another one. The ball comes to you. You control it, keep it close. Hard-running defenders rush upon you. The field is a mass of enemy jerseys. You look for a teammate, spot him, pass off. You run to him, take a return pass behind the defender. You pass the ball back to your teammate as he comes running by you. Suddenly he loses it to a defender's sliding tackle. Now the defense begins its attack. Now *you* are the defender. Where are they going with the ball? How can you cut off the pass? Can you risk committing yourself by rushing in on the ball and possibly leaving an open field behind you for a breakaway pass?

The action is constant. The motion is fluid, quick, sudden. One moment a serious attack threatens; the next moment everyone's running

Artistic shot of a ball, front lit, in isolation.

backward, trying to catch up with a reversal of the play. Your mind must always be focused, judging, deciding. And you're not alone. You're a member of a unit, a team. In a way, it's as if your self were extended into the bodies of all eleven players, in every corner of the field. You are they, and they are you. When you pass, you pass to another version of yourself.

And there's more. The *feeling* of kicking the ball. It's magical, it feels so good. It's addictive. The courage that's required. The incredible endurance, the ability to draw on reserves of energy when it seems there's not a single step left—to make the last push that marks the difference between mere performance and total involvement.

Soccer is unique among team sports in the degree of its unnaturalness. So many of the fundamental techniques and movements of soccer are in direct opposition to the body's instincts. It's as if the game were grounded in man's will to overcome himself and his limitations.

Most sports are forms of competitive play based on the skilled application of fairly primitive instinctual maneuvers. What could be more natural than swinging a stick with two hands or throwing a ball with one, as in baseball or cricket? Every caveman must have performed the same actions with his clubs and stones. Or basketball—a large object comes at you; you put up your hands and catch it; then you throw the ball at a target. Who couldn't imagine inventing some similar game himself?

Hockey is stick swinging (one must admit that skates are a technological intrusion); American football is ball throwing and catching, grabbing and subduing the enemy; ditto Rugby; tennis is stick swinging, swimming is survival, track is running and jumping and throwing—all natural acts, natural practices.

But look at soccer. Here, if a player puts up his hands to block a ball zooming fifty miles an hour right at his chest—the obvious instinctual act—he's penalized for it. Here, if a fast-moving object comes at a player's head, he's not supposed to do the natural thing and duck. He's supposed to hit it with his head! Absurd!

Even the basic kicks and traps are a perverse challenge to the body. The natural way for, say, a child to kick is with his toe. But in soccer you twist the leg unnaturally in order to kick accurately and powerfully with the instep, the outstep, or the side of the foot. Traps, in effect, are ways of catching the slippery ball with your feet or thighs or chest.

There's something dialectical about the sport, something that speaks forcefully about man's need to be more than he is. About man's need to take and subdue the other and to make it his own. When you watch a good player smoothly and fluidly performing all of these acts that the body was really not meant to perform, nothing could seem more natural. They are *made* natural.

This naturalness is at the heart of soccer. Fluid, organic movement is as necessary for the individual player as it is for the team. This flow of movement must be learned, like the flow of a dancer's movement, over years of practice and hard work. Many professional soccer players work out several hours a day in addition to team practice, just to keep their skills finely honed. Because it is impossible to achieve the developed naturalness, the flow, without acquiring and maintaining basic skills that are appropriately graceful, light, and subtle.

To be sure, a player must master ball-control skills, but that's not even half the story. In soccer, the team is everything. To take possession of the ball and to keep it moving, the players must relate to one another. They need to communicate verbally and through the language of motion, as close as lovers. A player must know exactly when a teammate will break to an open space and must be able to anticipate the move with confidence. No one player is less important than any other—the individual is subsumed into the moving whole. Each body is like a part of a single, greater body. Each mistake is a wound.

Forming and reforming, the team carves out space on the field. Passing is the name of the game. There's no room in soccer for the hotshot dribbler, the show-off. Great players are great not because they excel singly and in isolation, but because they catalyze and guide the rest of the players into a smoothly functioning unit. The best players are best at passing the ball to an open teammate.

Scoring? In a way scoring is not really the point. Scoring is the logical and inevitable result for a team that moves the ball, works the ball, and plays a controlled, strategic game. When a team performs according to principles in an organized, aggressive, and intelligent way, goals come. It's rare indeed when the final score does not reflect exactly how the game was played.

Time-lapse photo of a passing sequence.

2
A Short History of Soccer

In the beginning there must have been a bone, perhaps an old, light bird's skull. Or maybe it was a nest, or a dried piece of fruit, or a pinecone. Whatever the case, man must have begun to kick such things as soon as he learned to walk upright. The elements of soccer—running, kicking—are rooted in primal instincts of the body. Although the modern history of the game that we know as soccer extends only a little more than a hundred years into the human past, the origins of man's impulse to similar kinds of play go back to the very beginnings of mankind. Though the present game seems to have strictly British roots, we have records of something like soccer in the very earliest cultures. Many centuries before the birth of Christ the Chinese and Japanese played a team sport with a stuffed ball on the ground. Archaeologists tell us that the ancient Egyptians had balls that could have been used to play soccer. The ancient Greeks played a game called Espiros which seems to have borne a strong resemblance to what we now call Rugby.

Historians speculate that this Greek game was taken over by the Romans after they conquered the Greeks, just as the Romans appropriated much of Greek culture. It is indeed possible that the Romans brought Espiros to England after conquering it, but we have no sure evidence that they did.

What we *do* know is that, whether soccer was brought to England or arose there spontaneously as it had elsewhere, England was the womb of our modern game. In 1314 Edward II proclaimed the prohibition of a game which made "a great noise in the city caused by hustling over large balls." The serfs played this game in the streets, interfering with the course of feudal business.

By 1349 Edward III was calling the game football. His dislike of this activity was such that he threatened prison as punishment for those who engaged in it. The historical records on this subject are sketchy, so that we don't know precisely what this game of "football" was like. In all probability it was a hectic, chaotic, rough affair, much like Rugby. In any case not until many centuries later do we find a game

4

which disallowed the use of the hands and hacking at the opponent's legs.

"Football" continued as a grass roots form of play in England despite the official disapproval of both church and state until the nineteenth century. Organized institutions tried to prevent its growth, but the intrinsic appeal of the sport was too strong to be squelched by the higher social classes. It was a rough game, and many players were hurt, but it remained a favorite pastime.

Oddly, it was the schoolboy population which finally brought soccer under official sanction, legitimized it, and shaped it into the game we know today. In the early 1800s the English prep schools were in a turmoil. The students were undisciplined, rebelled constantly, and could not be taught. Part of their rebellion stemmed from the fact that they were not allowed to engage in sports, specifically football. The problem reached crisis proportions, and the educational authorities finally decided that even football was preferable to the anarchy which was overtaking them.

Thus football became, in effect, legalized. And with legalization came new rules. For if there had to be football, at least some order would be brought to it. The size of teams was limited, so that the game would not continue to be played as a violent free-for-all. Referees were used for the first time. A split developed, however, between a group that favored a game in which the hands could be used and a group that favored a game in which only the feet and the head were used. Rugby became the game of the former group, and the elite schools, such as Eton and Harrow, opted for the dribbling game, football (soccer).

Once football had taken a solid hold in the schools, it spread throughout the country, as prep school graduates continued to play on club teams. New rules of all sorts were introduced in the first half of the nineteenth century until, finally, in 1862, J. C. Thring of Cambridge University attempted to codify the disparate rules that had developed. He described the rules he formulated as the rules for "the simplest game," and they included prohibitions against throwing the ball (but not against catching it) and against kicking the opponent's legs.

Then, on October 26, 1863, the leading English clubs met in London to form the Football Association, whose goal was to regulate soccer throughout Britain. At this point the modern game of football (or, as we call it, soccer) began. The rules that were adopted were quite similar to those of today's game, except that the field could be up to 200 yards long and that a player was allowed to catch the ball and place it at his feet.

Soccer was an upper-class activity, a game for gentlemen, until 1882, when Blackburn, a working-class team, won the British championship for the first time. After that the game was ready to take its place as a sport for "everyman," and it did so quite rapidly. Professional leagues sprouted, and that, as it always does, injected a great growth stimulant into soccer. Whereas only 2,000 "gentlemen" watched the 1871 Cup Final match, over 110,000 were present at the 1901 match!

During the same period soccer was spreading, as a British export, throughout the world. Britain's worldwide influence was then perhaps at its all-time zenith. Britain's navy ruled the seas; its merchant marine dominated international trade routes; and its colonial empire embraced vast areas in all parts of the world. Wherever the British went, whether to Paris or Uruguay, they brought their "new" game with them.

Soccer, as we have noted, appeals to powerful motives that lie deep within people everywhere, no matter what their culture or language. No one was *forced* to play soccer, but millions of people took to the game because they were attracted to it on a level beyond words. Soccer became one of the major exports of British colonialism, appearing almost simultaneously in Europe, North and South America, and the Far East. By 1904 soccer was sufficiently entrenched internationally to give rise to the formation of the Fédération Internationale de Football Associations (FIFA) at a meeting in Paris. The purpose of FIFA was to standardize and control the rules of soccer all over the world, and to this day FIFA remains the preeminent world governing body of soccer.

During this period of relatively slow transportation among nations, international competition took place on a fairly limited scale. Only five countries were represented by soccer teams at the 1908 Olympics. By the time of the 1920 Olympics, twenty teams were represented, but the quality of Olympic play did not reflect the quality of soccer in virtually any of those countries. For only amateur players can participate in Olympic events, and by 1920 nearly every country had flourishing professional soccer leagues. The best soccer players were playing for money, not gold medals. To solve this problem, and to create an international competition whose *only* focus was soccer, FIFA decided to organize what quickly came to be called the World Cup.

Uruguay wanted to host the first World Cup as a celebration of the 100th anniversary of its independence. The European teams were reluctant to make a three-week boat trip (one way) in order to participate in a tournament of questionable value. But the small nation of Uruguay became the chosen site when it offered to build a new 100,000-seat stadium and to pay all the expenses of the tournament, including travel expenses for every team. For FIFA, short of funds and anxious to get a world championship off the ground, the offer was too good to pass up. Several major teams, including the British, refused to make the trip, but that first World Cup, in 1930, did indeed prove to be an international competition. Uruguay surprised the entire soccer world by defeating Argentina in the Final, completing the first round of an event that has become the most widely watched (and wagered on!) event in the sports world.

The rules of soccer have remained virtually unchanged for seventy-five years. The history of soccer has become a history of changes in tactics and strategies, as we shall see later in this book. But that has been true only in the rest of the world. Here in America, as most of us know by now, the history of soccer is just beginning. To be sure, soccer has been played on these shores for many years. But until the 1970s, you'd hardly have known it.

One common question about American soccer should be answered before we take a look at the development of the sport in this country. Why is soccer called soccer in the United States rather than football or *futbol* as it is known in the rest of the world? No one is absolutely certain about the reason for the name change, but one common guess is most probably right. English schoolboys had a habit of adding an *er* suffix to various words, as a kind of slang. Thus they didn't refer to Rugby as Rugby; they called it rugger. It should be remembered that the original name of soccer was association football. Most commentators believe that the term *soccer* derives from the addition of the schoolboy *er* to the abbreviation for *association* which was often used, *assoc*. From *assoc.* to *soc.* plus the *er* yields *soccer*.

Another interesting point: the famous 1869 Princeton-Rutgers "football" game was played under the rules of the London Football Association. This game, which is said to be the first game of American football ever played, was in fact a *soccer* game!

Still, until recently few people played soccer in this country. The game was always considered a sport for preppies, Ivy Leaguers, and immigrants. But times change. Although virtually nothing happened to American soccer for about a hundred years, the throttle has suddenly opened wide.

SOCCER U.S.A.

It is an intermittently rainy Wednesday evening at Giants Stadium, its tons of glistening white concrete perched incongruously atop New Jersey's vast turnpike marshes, in the new Meadowlands sports complex. The air is hot, humid, stifling, on the verge of a downpour. Still, over 30,000 undaunted soccer fans have shown up to watch the Cosmos take on the San Jose Earthquakes. Pele, the legendary Brazilian superstar whose presence has brought the game of soccer into its own in this country, won't be playing tonight. That doesn't matter. The fans don't care. They're here to watch *soccer*.

The crowd roars with the first kickoff, and it will not stop responding to the action until the last play is squeezed into the final second of the ninety nonstop minutes that make up a match. The wiry fullback Rildo has been trapped with the ball by three San Jose players, but he manages to feint and fake and shuffle and eke out a pass to Franz Beckenbauer (the West German star voted the best player in Europe last year and recently imported by the Cosmos). Though the fans are mostly white suburbanites, they chant approval in a Spanish accent, "*Reeeel-do, Reeeel-do!*"

The sport is chic now, and so is its international flavor. Beckenbauer, a six-footer and big by soccer standards, moves gracefully toward the San Jose goal, pushing the ball over to an open Tony Field (an English veteran). Field goes around one defender, fakes another out of position, then lofts the ball far across the Earthquake defense to the Italian star striker, Chinaglia. No quarterback calls these plays; no substitute rushes in with instructions from the coach. Soccer's a game of instinct. A groundswell cheer rises as Chinaglia approaches the goal, stalking for a score. Instead of shooting, he flips the ball through two defenders back to Field, who has broken clear toward the far goalpost. In a charged moment, Field, free and alone, slams the ball past a helpless Earthquake goalkeeper. The fans go wild. "AWWWWW-RRRRRIGHT," flashes the scoreboard, "AWWWWWRRRRRIGHT." These foreign athletes have become the new American sports heroes.

The crowd at Meadowlands is surprising in its composition—not the predominantly male, immigrant, or ethnic crowd you'd expect. To be sure, the Italians are here, and the Germans are here (soccer is the major sport in almost every country but ours), but the stands are full of all-American suburban kids—wide-eyed, glued to the action on the field, dressed in jackets covered with patches from the small-town teams they've played on: Scarsdale, Mineola, Poughkeepsie, Short Hills. Many of these kids are girls. In fact, many of the adult fans are women (women account for some 45 percent of NASL attendance). Soccer's new audience is clean-cut, affluent, "upscale" to the Madison Avenue types who are now following its progress quite seriously. And neither this new audience nor the phenomenal growth of the game is any accident. A strenuous public relations effort over the last eight years conducted by the North American Soccer League and its 18 franchised club managements is just now beginning to yield impressive results. As League Commissioner Phil Woosnam puts it in his now barely discernible

Welsh accent, "We've had to be soccer missionaries."

His converts do not exactly hail from the nation's inner cities. The new base for soccer is in the suburbs, surrounding what Woosnam calls the "all-American" cities, places like Dallas, Los Angeles, and Seattle. Eighty-six percent of soccer fans are under 44 years of age; 74 percent have attended college; more than half have annual family incomes of over $20,000. In unlikely towns like Tampa, bumper stickers and T-shirts announce that "soccer is a kick in the grass." In Minneapolis–St. Paul, swarms of suburbanites descend on the stadium parking lot hours before gametime for tailgating picnics—it's a family affair—and linger hours after the game, when team players come out to mingle with the fans. In Los Angeles, young rooters might be treated to the sight of rock singer and soccer aficionado Elton John cheering on the Aztecs, of which he owns a major share.

Advertisers have been quick to pick up on the new American pastime. Now, on television, we see towheaded suburban kids—somehow each one looks like a Kennedy—earnestly dribbling and passing and closing in for a shot on goal. Then, a Coke. A print ad in *Barron's* shows an "upscale" woman standing next to her new Mercedes, which is parked next to the soccer field where her two Etonesque boys have just been hard at it.

The *image* of soccer in this country has changed, has been made to change, and the change in image, like so much else in America, has brought success. As former Cosmos coach Gordon Bradley put it, "We're not offering a fad. This is a genuine sport, the top sport in 147 countries around the world. But we had to create an image to get Americans—the most sports-minded country—to accept soccer."

How did soccer move from the sandlots of immigrant areas into the razzle-dazzle mainstream world of major league professionalism and national television? The real thrust came from a handful of men who loved soccer and a challenge. Among these men were LaMar Hunt, of the wealthy Texas Hunt family, who owns the Dallas Tornado in the NASL (he also owns the American Football League Kansas City

Chiefs); Clive Toye, former president of the Cosmos, who brought Pele to this country (Pele himself was one of the handful); and the ever-running NASL commissioner, Woosnam. Let's follow the story.

In the middle sixties the business of sports began to boom on all fronts. Tickets for professional football, basketball, and hockey games grew scarce. Tennis and golf players found themselves waiting in line to use facilities that were inadequate to meet the demand. Television had discovered, or rediscovered, professional sports and began pouring money into broadcasting contracts. At relatively low cost, a network could hold the attention of a large audience for one, two, even three hours while the network's advertisers sold the fans beer, razors, autos, soap. As TV money juiced up sports income and broadened the ticket-buying base, teams that had been glamour toys for the rich suddenly began making the rich even richer. Whoever had a sporting event to sell to television had the proverbial goods.

People already involved in professional sport now saw the opportunity to develop a new sports product for the media. What they had in sight was soccer, the behemoth of sport, number one in the world with a global audience of over a *billion*. Never mind that Americans couldn't have cared less about the game at the time. Americans loved sport, and once exposed to the beauties and excitement of soccer, they would become hooked. How could a billion soccer fans be wrong?

In 1967 two professional soccer leagues were formed, the United States Association and the National Professional Soccer League. A network contract with CBS appeared with remarkable speed for a sport so new. Having imported rather average professional teams from Europe and South America to provide the action, the new team owners sat back and prepared to savor their slice of the American soccer pie.

But soccer proved to be more like a pop tart than a pie. No one came to the games. Sometimes there were more stadium personnel than paying fans. American football was ascendant, and baseball was solidly entrenched. Who gave a damn about the immigrant sport?

In 1968 the owners tried again, merging the two leagues into one and renaming it the North American Soccer League. But at that time even one league proved to be one league too many. Twelve of its seventeen teams dropped out after the 1968 season, leaving the NASL as an operating professional league with an absurd total of five teams. Woosnam, the newly appointed commissioner and a former soccer star himself, was still convinced that soccer could make it. As coach of the Atlanta franchise in 1967–68 he had seen crowds of more than 20,000 coming to games in a city that had absolutely no soccer background and a negligible immigrant population.

To an outsider, though, the situation in 1969 looked patently hopeless. Most of the original teams were gone, having lost millions. Only the diehards remained, the true believers. Among them was LaMar Hunt, who felt that he had an obligation to the people he'd begun with, and who, as part owner of one of the great American fortunes, lent credibility to the apparently incredible enterprise. The mere mention of his name caused potential franchise buyers to think twice about what seemed to be a ridiculous investment. Hunt had no special background in soccer. "I was just another businessman trying to build a show business attraction," he says.

And the drawing power of the league did indeed build up. The previous CBS television exposure had helped bring soccer to the American hinterlands; young people had begun to play it; and now, finally, they wanted to see the real thing, in the flesh. Although the crowds were still relatively small in the first few years after 1969 (average attendance was about 8,000, and 20,000 was terrific), the popularity of the sport grew sufficiently to interest other entrepreneurs with eyes on the future. During the same years, as communities and schools discovered that soccer was an inexpensive and safe sport that provided great conditioning and athletic opportunities to youths of both sexes and all ages and sizes, "the simplest game" began to appear with increasing frequency on the playing fields of suburbia. By the winter of 1975, with Woosnam covering 250,000 miles a year out selling soccer franchises to anyone with money who'd listen, the NASL had expanded to 20 teams. In the meantime, registered soccer-playing young people had jumped from perhaps 50,000 in 1965 to half a million.

The teams were still losing money, though. Soccer was developing some momentum, but its future as a major professional sport seemed doubtful to all but the inner circle of soccer promoters. The game needed some kind of push, some oomph, before it could really break into the American consciousness.

Soccer needed what every other sport had, a superstar—someone who could capture the imagination of the nation's youth, the broadcast media, and the press. In the spring of 1975, after years of cajoling and negotiation, Clive Toye, president of the Cosmos, succeeded in signing the world's most famous, highest paid, and perhaps *best* athlete to play for his struggling New York franchise.

Pele, the Black Panther, broke soccer wide open in this country. The papers were full of his multi-million-dollar contract. Media executives sat up at their desks. What's this? What's the world's greatest soccer player doing in America? No one with even the remotest interest in sports could fail to be aware of the presence of a great new athlete. It was only natural that thousands would want to see his act and the stage on which he played. Wherever Pele went, attendance more than doubled. Stadia which had never filled for soccer had to turn fans away at the gate.

Signing Pele was a coup for the Cosmos and for the NASL, but it had been no easy matter. Toye and Woosnam first contacted Pele at an exhibition game in Jamaica in 1971. At that time Pele was looking toward retirement, and Toye and Woosnam suggested that he might come to play in America as a kind of soccer ambassador. In 1971 no great soccer star could take an American offer seriously, but Toye and Woosnam are men who don't give up until an issue is utterly and irredeemably dead. Toye met with Pele again and again, in Sao Pãulo, in Rome, in Munich, in Brussels. The global courtship lasted three years, and it included over 100 direct contacts, along with countless letters and telex messages. Pele was the king of the most popular sport on earth, and Toye finally prevailed by appealing to Pele's regal instincts

toward immortality. "You can go down in history as the man who truly brought soccer to the United States, the one major country in which it has not caught on," Toye told Pele. For a humble man who'd started his career by kicking around a ball of twine, this was an attractive idea. A six-year contract, including three years as a player and three as a public relations figure for Warner Communications (owner of the Cosmos), a complicated offshore tax-free incorporation deal, and at least $5 million must have helped Pele decide.

Even so, the matter became a delicate problem in international relations. Pele was Brazil's pride and joy—the Brazilian government had already declared him a national treasure—and the Brazilian soccer establishment, government, soccer fans, and press had to be convinced that this was more than a *norteamericano* buy-out. This task was finally accomplished through a blitz (in Warner's best communications style) of public relations releases, press meetings, government announcements, repeated statements by Pele himself, and even the intercession of soccer fan and then Secretary of State Henry Kissinger. Kissinger argued that having Pele come to the United States would be a great thing for U.S.-Brazilian relations, and shortly afterward the Brazilian government approved Pele's move to its most important hemispheric ally.

The growth of soccer that had been some ten years in the making spurted ahead another ten years on a single night in June 1975. Godlike, Pele descended from the sky in a helicopter that landed at funky Randall's Island stadium (then the home field of the Cosmos). The fans mobbed him, as they continued to do for his three seasons with the Cosmos, trying to touch him, to see him.

On the field, even an out-of-shape Pele could toy with ball and opponent like a Harlem Globetrotter. A Greek chorus of oohs and aahs sang from the stands as Pele gently and precisely pushed the ball through his opponent's legs, or bounced it seven or eight times on his own thighs as he ran past three defenders, or reached out and plucked a chest-high pass from midair with his *foot*, laying the obedient ball quietly before him.

American soccer had finally got its Joe Na-

TABLE 1
ALL TIME NASL RECORDS

Individual Offensive Records

Most scoring points, season	69—(30 goals, 9 assists) John Kowalik, Chicago Mustangs '68 (28 games)
Most scoring points, game	12—Giorgio Chinaglia (New York) vs. Miami 8/10/76
Most scoring points, one-half	8—Andy Provan (Philadelphia) vs. Washington 5/4/74 (4 goals); Giorgio Chinaglia (New York) vs. Miami 8/10/76 (4 goals)
Most goals, season	30—John Kowalik (Chicago) '68; Cirilo Fernandez. (San Diego) '68
Most goals, game	5—Ron Moore (Chicago) vs. Vancouver 6/24/77; Giorgio Chinaglia (New York) vs. Miami 8/10/76; Steve David (Miami) vs. Washington 6/20/75
Most goals, one-half	4—Andy Provan (Philadelphia) vs. Washington 5/4/74; Giorgio Chinaglia (New York) vs. Miami 8/10/76
Most consecutive games scoring a goal	10—Steve David (Los Angeles) '77
Fastest goal	:21—Willie Mfum (New York) vs. Rochester 8/2/71
Latest goal	90:00—Ilija Mitic (San Jose) vs. St. Louis 5/2/75
Shortest time to score two goals	1:00—Morrie Diane (Washington) vs. Baltimore 7/27/74; Miguel Perrichon (Toronto) vs. Montreal 8/7/73
Shortest time to score three goals	11:00—Willie Mfum (New York) vs. Rochester 6/9/71
Shortest time to score four goals	35:00—Andy Provan (Philadelphia) vs. Washington 5/4/74
Most goals on penalty kicks, season	8—Keith Eddy (New York) '76
Most goals on penalty kicks, game	2—Manfred Eickerling (Boston) vs. Rochester 7/20/74; Barry Lynch (Atlanta) vs. Lanerossi Vicenza (Italy) 6/15/71
Most penalty kicks missed, season	2—Charlie Mitchell (Rochester) '72; Carlos Metidieri (Rochester) '71
Most assists, season	18—George Best (Los Angeles) '77; Pele (New York) '76
Most assists, game	4—Vito Dimitrijevic (Cosmos) vs. Toronto 6/5/77; Roberto Aguirre (Miami) vs. New York 6/14/74; Miguel Perrichon (Toronto) vs. Miami 5/6/72
Most assists, one-half	3—Alan Wooler (Boston) vs. New York 8/3/75; Roberto Aguirre (Miami) vs. New York 6/14/74; Ian Filby (Montreal) vs. Rochester 7/17/73; Miguel Perrichon (Toronto) vs. Miami 5/6/72
Most consecutive games with an assist	5—George Best (Los Angeles) '77; Carlos Metidieri (Rochester) '71

Goalkeeper Records

Most goals allowed, season	52—Peter Fox (Hawaii) '77
Best goals against average, season	0.62—Bob Rigby (Philadelphia) '73; Mirko Stojanovic (Dallas) '71
Fewest goals allowed, season	8—Bob Rigby (Philadelphia) '73
Most shut-outs, season	12—Lincoln Phillips (Washington) '70
Most consecutive shut-outs, season	4—Zeljko Bilecki (Toronto) '75; Ken Cooper (Dallas) '74; Claude Campos (Rochester) '74 & '73
Most consecutive minutes without allowing a goal, one season	476—Claude Campos (Rochester) '72
Most saves, game	22—Mike Winter (St. Louis) vs. Rochester 5/27/73
Fewest saves, game	0—Tony Chursky (Seattle) vs. San Jose 6/4/76; Dave Landry (Portland) vs. San Diego 6/2/76; Zeljko Bilecki (Toronto) vs. Rochester 7/6/75
Fewest saves, game, both teams	3—Zeljko Bilecki (Toronto) 2, Jim May (Rochester) 1, 7/23/75
Most saves, game, without allowing a goal	21—Sam Nusum (Montreal) vs. Miami 5/5/73
Most minutes played, one season	2386—Arnie Mausser (Vancouver) '77

Team General Records

Most games won, season	19—Ft. Lauderdale '77; Oakland '67
Highest winning percentage, season	75%—Tampa Bay '76 (18 of 24)
Fewest games won, season	2—Baltimore '69; Dallas '68
Lowest winning percentage, season	6%—Dallas '68 (2 of 32)
Most consecutive games won	8—Los Angeles '74; Oakland '68
Most consecutive games without a loss (regulation time)	14—Dallas '74
Most games lost, season	26—Dallas '68
Most consecutive games lost	11—Hartford '75
Most consecutive games without a victory	22—Dallas '68
Most games tied, season (regulation time)	12—New York '68
Highest percentage of tied games, season (regulation time)	47%—Toronto '73 (9 of 19)
Fewest games tied, season (regulation time)	1—Baltimore '69
Lowest percentage of tied games, season (regulation time)	6%—Baltimore '69 (1 of 16)
Most tie-breakers, season	9—Vancouver '74
Most tie-breakers won, season	6—Miami '74
Most tie-breakers lost, season	5—Vancouver '74; Miami '74
Most consecutive tie-breakers won, season	6—Miami '74
Most consecutive tie-breakers lost, season	3—Dallas '77; Minnesota '77; Dallas '74; Boston '74; St. Louis '74

Team Offensive Records

Most goals scored, season	71—Oakland '68
Highest goals per game average, season	3.3—Kansas City '69 (53 goals in 16 games)
Fewest goals scored, season	15—Dallas '72
Lowest goals per game average, season	88—Dallas '68 (28 in 32 games)
Most goals, game	9—New York (vs. Washington) 6/29/75; Oakland (vs. St. Louis) 7/26/67
Most goals, game, both teams	12—Toronto 8, Chicago 4, 8/27/68
Largest margin of victory	9—Oakland (9-0) vs. St. Louis 7/26/67
Most games scoring 5 or more goals, season	4—Kansas City '68
Most games scoring 4 or more goals, season	8—Oakland '68
Most games scoring 3 or more goals, season	14—Oakland '68
Most games scoring 2 or more goals, season	21—San Diego '68, Cleveland '68
Most consecutive games scoring 1 or more goals, season	24—Minnesota '76; Chicago '68
Most goals, two consecutive games	12—San Jose '76, New York '75
Most goals, three consecutive games	15—Tampa Bay '76; Kansas City '68
Most goals, four consecutive games	18—Chicago '76
Most goals, five consecutive games	21—Chicago '76; Tampa Bay '76
Most goals, tie game (regulation time)	8—Chicago at Atlanta 6/4/67; Toronto at St. Louis 8/22/67
Shortest time to score two goals, game	:15—Ft. Lauderdale (vs. Dallas) 6/25/77
Shortest time to score three goals, game	2:00—Philadelphia (vs. Rochester) 6/22/73; Toronto (vs. Vera Cruz-Mexico) 7/1/73
Shortest time to score four goals, game	13:31—Seattle (vs. Hawaii) 8/4/77
Most games held scoreless	11—Montreal '71
Fewest games held scoreless	0—Minnesota '76; New York '76; Seattle '75
Most consecutive games held scoreless	5—Miami '76; Denver '74
Most consecutive minutes held scoreless	523—Denver '74
Most own goals, season	4—Dallas '77
Most shots, game	45—Hawaii (vs. Los Angeles) 7/22/77
Most shots, game, both teams	66—Baltimore (42) vs. San Jose (24) 5/24/76; New York (43) vs. Rochester (23) 6/9/71
Fewest shots, game	1—Rochester (vs. Toronto) 7/6/75
Fewest shots, game, both teams	16—Vancouver (9) vs. Hartford (7) 5/25/75; Dallas (9) vs. Toronto (7) 5/5/73; Rochester (5) vs. Hearts-Scortland (11) 6/9/71
Most penalty kicks, game	2—Several games
Most penalty kicks, game, both teams	3—Dallas (2) vs. San Antonio (1) 4/18/75; Boston (2) vs. Rochester (1) 7/20/74; Dallas (2) vs. New York (1) 8/11/73; Atlanta (2) vs. Lanerossi Vincenza-Italy (1) 6/15/71
Most penalty kicks, season	8—New York '76
Most penalty kicks missed, season	3—Rochester '72

Team Defensive Records

Most goals allowed, season	109—Dallas '68
Highest average goals per game allowed, season	3.4—Dallas (109 in 32 games) '68
Fewest goals allowed, season	14—Philadelphia '73
Lowest average goals per game allowed	74—Philadelphia (14 in 19 games) '73
Most goals allowed, game	9—St Louis (vs. Oakland) 7/26/67; Washington (vs. New York) 6/29/75
Most games holding the opposition scoreless	12—Washington '70
Most consecutive games holding opposition scoreless	4—Toronto '75; Dallas '74; Rochester '74; Rochester '72
Most games holding opposition to one goal or none	18—Philadelphia '73
Most consecutive games holding opposition to one goal or none	11—Los Angeles '67
Most games holding opposition to two goals or fewer	27—Oakland '67
Most penalty kicks against, season	8—Toronto '71

Attendance

Largest attendance, regular season	62,394—New York (Giants Stadium) vs. Tampa Bay 6/19/77
Largest attendance, playoff game	77,691—New York (Giants Stadium) vs. Ft. Lauderdale 8/14/77
Largest attendance, international game	75,641—Santos vs. New York Cosmos (Giants Stadium) 10/1/77
Largest total attendance, season, one club	443,847—New York (13 games) '77
Largest average attendance, season, one club	34,142—New York (13 games) '77
Largest number of sellouts, season	7—Seattle (Memorial Stadium) '75, capacity 14,876
Largest league attendance, regular season	3,172,780—'77 (234 games)
Largest league attendance, total	3,674,638—'77 (251 games)
Largest average per game attendance, season	13,559—'77 (234 games)
Largest average per game attendance, total	14,640—'77 (251 games—includes playoffs)
Largest U.S. soccer crowd	77,691—New York (Giants Stadium) vs. Ft. Lauderdale 8/14/77

TABLE 2
PLAYOFF RECORDS

Individual Playoff Records

Most Total Points in Playoff Games, Career	20—Giorgio Chinaglia (Cosmos)
Most Playoff Points, One Season	20—Giorgio Chinaglia (Cosmos) 1977
Most Playoff Points, One Game	7—Giorgio Chinaglia (Cosmos) vs. Ft. Lauderdale 8/14/77 (3 goals, 1 assist)
Most Goals in Playoffs, Career	9—Giorgio Chinaglia (Cosmos)
Fastest Goal in Playoffs	1:30—Joe Jelinek (Boston Minutemen) vs. Baltimore Bays, 1974
Latest Goal in Playoffs	176:00—Carlos Metidieri (Rochester Lancers) vs. Dallas Tornado 9/1/71
Shortest Time to Score Two Goals	:47—Des Backos and Charlie Cooke (Los Angeles Aztecs) vs. Dallas 8/17/77
Shortest Time to Score Three Goals	3:29—Miro Rys, Des Backos, Charlie Cooke (Los Angeles Aztecs) vs. Dallas 8/17/77
Most Playoff Assists, One Season	7—Steve Hunt (Cosmos) 1977
Most Playoff Assists, Career	7—Steve Hunt (Cosmos)
Most Assists, One Game	3—Steve Hunt (Cosmos) vs. Tampa Bay 8/10/77

Goalkeepers Records

Most Goals Allowed in Playoffs, Career	18—Ken Cooper (Dallas)
Best Goals Against Average, One Season	0.00—Paul Hammond (Tampa Bay) 1975 (3 games); Bob Rigby (Philadelphia) 1973 (2 games)
Best Goals Against Average, Career (need 270 minutes)	0.69—Zeljko Bilecki (Toronto) (5 goals, 652 minutes)
Fewest Goals Allowed, One Season	0—Bob Rigby (Philadelphia) 1973; Paul Hammond (Tampa Bay) 1975
Most Shutouts, Career	3—Paul Hammond (Tampa Bay); Ken Cooper (Dallas); Zeljko Bilecki (Toronto); Jack Brand (Rochester)
Most Saves, One Game	17—Mirko Stojanovic (Dallas) vs. Rochester, 9/14/71; Jerry Sularz (Cosmos) vs. Dallas, 8/15/73
Fewest Saves, One Game	1—Jack Brand (Rochester) vs. Toronto 8/13/77; Jack Brand (Rochester) vs. Cosmos 8/22/77
Fewest Saves, One Game by Two Teams	4—Dallas and Los Angeles, 8/18/76; San Jose and Los Angeles, 8/10/77
Most Goals Allowed, One Season	10—Gordon Banks (Ft. Lauderdale) 1977

Team Records

Most Playoff Games Won	9—Cosmos (2 in '72, 1 in '76, 6 in '77)
Best Winning Percentage	1.000—Philadelphia (two wins in two games)
Lowest Winning Percentage	0.000—Vancouver (0 wins in two games)
Most Consecutive Games Won	6—Cosmos 1977
Most Playoff Games Participated In	15—Dallas

Team Offensive Records

Most Playoff Goals, Career	28—Cosmos
Highest Average Goals Per Game, Career	2.25—Miami/Ft. Lauderdale (9 goals in 4 games)
Most Goals, One Game	8—Cosmos (vs. Ft. Lauderdale) 8/14/77
Most Goals, Two Teams, One Game	—Cosmos 8, Ft. Lauderdale 3, 8/14/77 at Giants Stadium
Most Games Scoring One or More Goals	12—Dallas
Most Penalty Shot Goals	1—Joe Jelinek (Cosmos) vs. St. Louis, 8/26/72; Jim Fryatt (Philadelphia) vs. Toronto, 8/18/73; Tommy Ord (Seattle) vs. Minnesota, 8/17/77
Most Shots, One Game	38—Portland (vs. Seattle) 8/12/75
Fewest Shots, One Game	6—San Jose (vs. Minnesota) 8/28/76
Fewest Shots, Two Teams	21—Minnesota (15) vs. San Jose (6) 8/25/76
Most Shots, Two Teams	55—Cosmos (31) at Ft. Lauderdale (24) 8/17/77; Cosmos (29) vs. Seattle (26) 8/28/77
Most Games Held Scoreless	4—Toronto
Fewest Games Held Scoreless	0—Philadelphia (2 games)

Team Defensive Records

Most Goals Allowed, Career	23—Dallas
Fewest Goals Allowed, One Season	0—Tampa Bay (3 games) 1975
Most games Held Opposition Scoreless	4—Dallas, Seattle
Most Games Held Opposition to One Goal or Less	9—Cosmos
Most Goals Allowed, One Season	11—Ft. Lauderdale (2 games) 1977

Attendance Records

Largest Playoff Attendance	77,691—Cosmos (Giants Stadium) vs. Ft. Lauderdale 8/14/77
Largest Playoff Total Attendance, One Season	501,858—1977 (17 games)
Largest Playoff Average Attendance	29,521—1977 (17 games)
Largest Team Total Attendance, One Season	212,410—Cosmos 1977 (3 games)
Largest Average Per Game Attendance, One Team, One Season	70,803—Cosmos 1977

TABLE 3
NASL ALL-TIME LEADING SCORERS
(through 1977)

No.	Player (Present or Last NASL Team)	Games	Goals	Assists	Points
1	Ilija Mitic (San Jose)	147	96	34	226
2	Warren Archibald (Rochester)	162	58	39	155
3	Carlos Metidieri (Boston)	129	61	28	150
4	Paul Child (San Jose)	121	61	26	148
5	Leroy Deleon (San Jose)	141	56	32	144
6	Steve David (Los Angeles)	77	63	12	138
7	Derek Smethurst (Tampa Bay)	67	57	12	126
8	Randy Horton (Hartford)	89	51	23	125
9	Kaizer Motaung (Denver)	105	50	18	118
10	Manfred Seissler (Montreal)	87	43	27	113
11	Willie Roy (Chicago)	99	42	29	113
12	Art Welch (Washington)	171	38	34	110
13	Casey Frankiewicz (St. Louis)	110	44	20	108
14	Tommy Ord (Seattle)	97	42	19	103
15	Cirilo "Pepe" Fernandez (Seattle)	75	42	18	102
16	Kyle Rote, Jr. (Dallas)	100	36	27	99
17	John Kowalik (Chicago)	47	40	12	92
18	Pat McBride (St. Louis)	175	32	26	90
19	Giorgio Chinaglia (Cosmos)	43	34	19	87
20	Pele (Cosmos)	56	31	25	87
21	Eli Durante (Rochester)	170	29	26	84
22	Ade Coker (Minnesota)	73	33	16	82
23	Mike Renshaw (Dallas)	147	23	32	78
24	George Best (Los Angeles)	43	26	25	77
25	Al Trost (St. Louis)	108	28	19	75
26	Mike Stojanovic (Rochester)	48	31	12	74
27	Stewart Scullion (Portland)	66	28	18	74
28	Iris DeBrito (Denver)	68	29	15	73
29	Jorge Siega (New York)	109	21	29	71
30	Alan Willey (Minnesota)	43	30	8	68
31	Gene Geimer (Chicago)	83	26	16	68
32	Peter Silvester (Washington)	65	27	12	66
33	Dave Butler (Seattle)	74	27	10	64
34	John Coyne (Hartford)	62	22	19	63
35	Denny Vaninger (Ft. Lauderdale)	70	23	16	62
36	Freddie Mwila (Atlanta)	119	25	12	62

math, its Muhammad Ali, its Babe Ruth. In fact, it had gone the other sports one better, for Pele had proved himself in the stadia of the world. His was a name sportscasters could pronounce (it's *pay-lay*), and his style was sweet, humble. He exuded an almost religious goodness ("Soccer is life," he said. "All men must work together."), coming off as the kind of clean-cut hero that had practically vanished since the great liberation from all that in the sixties. And he got his press. Cosmos attendance soared at home and on the road, to an average of nearly 40,000 per game in 1977. People who'd never seen a soccer match before came out to watch the superstar Pele. It didn't matter that he was out of retirement and supposedly over the hill—he popped up everywhere on the field without ever seeming to move his legs. (In this game where running is everything, one imagines Pele coming back to the locker room cool as a cucumber, dry as a fresh towel.) American schoolchildren and pros alike finally saw how the game was supposed to be played.

Soccer was growing before Pele came, but it was as the mere starter motor for a jet engine. As a missionary, Pele succeeded where no one else could. On June 19, 1977, over 62,000 fans packed into Giants Stadium to watch him and the other ten Cosmos defeat the Tampa Bay Rowdies. It was a record crowd for soccer in this country *and* a record crowd for a summer sporting event in New York. With tears in his eyes Pele proclaimed after the game, "This is what I came for." And June 19 was no fluke. The following Sunday, the Cosmos attracted 57,000 fans, outdrawing a Yankees baseball game just across the river. Later, in August, crowds of over 75,000 filled the stadium twice.

On existing momentum alone, soccer will soon be a major sport on the order of football, baseball, and basketball. Now that Pele has played here, no world class player can think himself too good to come to America. (Europeans used to think that U.S. soccer was a joke and a circus. But 75,000 paying customers means that it is no longer a joke.) Indeed the NASL has become littered with great international stars: Beckenbauer, Chinaglia, George Best, Eusebio, Rodney Marsh, Derek Smethurst—players who are living legends in

their home countries. By League rule, Americans play on all teams, but there are few American standouts. It will take quite a few years before our level of play is up to international standards. Nevertheless, Woosnam claims that within ten years "not only will soccer be the number one sport in the U.S., we will also become the major soccer center of the world. America will win the World Cup. More people will watch and play soccer here than in any other country. It's a question," he adds, "of better marketing from here on in."

Soccer will grow because of its intrinsic attractions (exciting, safe, cheap, open to both men and women of average build) and because soccer club owners stand to make a rather large fortune if they are successful. Franchises are still inexpensive, perhaps the only bargain left in sports. Right now (1977), you can buy a franchise for only $250,000 cash plus a reserve of about $1,000,000 to cover start-up costs and losses for the first few years. As crowds grow to the point where average attendance exceeds 50,000 per game—which is a near-term probability for a few clubs—a team's average net income from ticket sales, concessions, and television might come to $1-2 million each year. That's comparable to what an NFL football club earns, and it represents an annual return on investment of more than 300 percent.

The real payoff, though, is in franchise value. Sports franchises such as NFL football clubs sell for ten to fifteen times their annual earnings. This means that in a few years (five to ten by most projections) a club might be worth $20-30 million, a cool 10,000 percent return. Toye claims that the Cosmos would be a quick sale, if they were for sale, at $5 million today. The value of the club in five years, with sellout crowds for twenty games and postseason European tours, is anyone's guess. The Cosmos could well become the most valuable sports franchise in the world. Yet only six years ago Warner Communications, then National Kinney, purchased the club for $10,000.

Obviously, if the club owners have anything to say about it, every youngster in this country is going to learn how to dribble. The club owners have taken a thoroughly businesslike approach to the sport, modeling their operations on the solid success of the National Football League. Clinics with team stars are held for kids. Free tickets go out to Boy Scouts and Girl Scouts. Bumper stickers appear as if for a political campaign. Public relations staffs churn out a stream of releases showing how much fun soccer is to play and watch. Local fans learn how to pronounce names like Vitomir Dimitrijevic and Ace Ntsoelengoe.

A swing toward soccer is surely in evidence, and a greater swing seems inevitable. Though sports are hardly our highest priority social concern, the swing toward soccer is probably a good thing for everyone. A sport that does not need *protective* equipment, that does not encase you in armor, has got to take us in a more positive direction than the slamming and banging and snorting and anger of football. As the global village becomes a reality, it seems fitting that we join the rest of the villagers in their free-flowing, nonlinear game.

Then, too, soccer may well become the game symbolic of our most crucial social change—the emergence of women. Considering the level of conditioning demonstrated by women in Olympic competition, it is already clear, contends Woosnam, that women can develop sufficient endurance to play soccer at any level. As more women learn the necessary ball-control skills, there is no reason why they can't compete on the same playing field with men. Some body contact is inevitable in soccer, and it remains to be seen whether or not women will be strong enough to deal with men when the ball is contested. But it is entirely conceivable that women and men will play together on interscholastic and intercollegiate teams. And it is not impossible that one day a woman will play alongside the next Pele or Beckenbauer on a North Amer-

ican Soccer League team. "Time is all it takes," says Woosnam. "Girls are now beginning to show real skills, real ball control."

TIPS FROM THE STARS

At different points in this book you will come across "tips from the stars," comments by North American Soccer League and U.S. National Team players (representing the United States in international competition but not in the Olympics) on how they play the game and on how they think it should be played. We interviewed many of these players especially for this book, and we're very grateful for their assistance.

We focus on *American* players, for it takes an American to understand the needs of the many fans and participants who are new to soccer in this country. America will have its own style of play (aggressive and hard running), which is just beginning to emerge in international competition, and these are the players who will help to mold that style.

On occasion the players disagree with one another and with certain remarks in the main text. This is as it should be. Wouldn't the world be a boring place if there were no disagreements? In soccer, as in any other field, no two people have precisely the same opinions. Even so, it is amazing how much the majority of soccer players and soccer writers *do* seem to agree on the important ideas about soccer. Goalies Alan Mayer and Arnold Mausser are quoted together because they were interviewed together and because during the interview they agreed with each other on everything!

Rather than recite the pertinent facts about each star each time his tips are quoted, we'll give the facts here, just once.

3
Skills and Ball Control

Ball control and soccer are synonymous. The major challenge of soccer is controlling the ball without the use of your hands. In that sense, soccer is ball control and ball control is soccer. Not speed afoot, not power in the kick, not bravery or muscle, not even the ability to make a spectacular play (though all of these things count). The game is simply ball control.

A ball is not a round object. A ball is a piece of *space*, *enclosed* by sewn leather in such a way as to make it look like a round object. But it's really space. Inside the ball, what do you have? You have space. If you focus on controlling the space *inside* the ball you'll find that the outer ball, the leather, will obey you as its master. This is true in every aspect of ball control. The ball must not be experienced as an alien object. It is simply a bit of enclosed space, a pressurized nothingness. When you kick, or when you trap, you kick or trap the space, not the ball. This way of understanding the ball helps you to receive it softly, to dribble it with confidence, and to kick it as your slave, not your enemy.

To control a ball well, you must learn to feel friendly toward it. Most beginning players feel antagonistic toward the ball, because it never quite does what they want it to. That's a matter of practice and work, of course, like any other skill. But you can't grow and develop if you feel that the ball is a source of frustration, that it is there to foil you. It isn't. It's just a ball, a piece of space. And you can conquer the difficulty of controlling it if you *believe* that you can. But when you see the ball as The Great Frustrator, when you see it as having some kind of magical power that limits your ability to master it, you limit yourself. It's surprising how many players secretly feel this way—that they can go only so far in controlling the ball and no farther. When this attitude develops, players stop trying to improve their game. When you stop trying to improve, the ball has defeated you.

A ball bounces because it's made of space, because it's light. So the first thing you have to do to acquire any ball-control skill is to *get light* too. Soccer is played on the toes, not the heels. There is a basic soccer position that keeps you in readiness for the application of any skill you may have to use. The idea is to keep light so that you can move quickly. Think of gravity as the enemy—but one that you can outwit to a certain extent by maintaining yourself in the basic position.

THE BASIC POSITION

1. *Your weight is on your toes.* This doesn't mean that you have to hike up and point like a ballet dancer—being up on the ball of your foot is close enough to being up on your toes. The main point is that your weight is pitched slightly forward and that *none* of it rests on your heels. If it helps you to actually raise your heels off the ground a bit too, that's fine.

2. *Your knees are slightly bent.* If you stand up straight and stiff, your knees are "locked." In order to make a move, you have to "unlock" them first. Standing with knees slightly bent, however, you're ready for immediate action. You may never have noticed it, but your knees always bend when you start to move. Why not be ready for movement by *starting out* with the knees bent? Then, too, by bending your knees slightly, you automatically shift your weight forward and onto your toes and the ball of the foot. Think of a runner on the starting blocks— knees bent, weight forward, on his toes. There is no need for a soccer player to crouch like that, but the basic principles still apply.

If your knees are not bent and you send your weight to the front of your feet, you upset your center of gravity. You're unstable that way, ripe for a stumble when you start to kick or trap or run. Your body weight is not sufficiently mobile. By bending your knees, you lower your weight to compensate for shifting it onto your toes— you maintain stability.

3. *Your legs are twelve to twenty-four inches apart.* This brings your center of gravity still lower, facilitating quick and easy movement. From a lower stance you can swing your body right and left, covering far less distance than would be required if you were stiff and upright.

4. *Your arms are held slightly up and out.* Like the tightrope walker's pole, our arms are a balancing mechanism. When you turn or you make a fast movement, notice how you lead into the turn or movement, not with your first

step, but with your *arm.* Your arms and hands are very useful in helping to create fast, fluid movement. They lead your body. So don't allow them to flop by your side or to stay stiff in some habitual position. You can't control the ball in soccer with your hands, but you *can* use your hands to control your body. The body's an integrated organism. Even when you play with your feet, every part of your body must do its share.

So remember the basic position for all of your ball-control skills:

1. Weight on your toes (or the ball of the foot).
2. Knees slightly bent.
3. Legs one to two feet apart.
4. Arms held slightly up and out, ready to lead a movement or to create balance.

Try ball-control skills from a stiff and heavy position, and then try them starting from the loose and light basic position. You'll see that if you begin light you stay light, all through your move, and that you do whatever you're trying to do much better. After all, you're trying to control space and to move in space—you've got to be light, just as space is.

A player can move right or left most rapidly—from the basic position—lowered weight is easier to shift.

TIPS FROM THE STARS: THE GREAT PLAYER

To become a good player you've got to know your skills first of all, and you need speed and strength. But just as important are discipline and intelligence. Playing with your head means a lot on the field—you can compensate for lack of speed with intelligence by making split-second decisions.

Steve Ralbovsky

The great player is Pele. A majority of the things he does are a result of balance and agility, but above all Pele's greatness is due to his *awareness*. When Pele gets the ball he already knows who is where and what he is going to do with the ball. That is what makes the difference—not Pele's speed or skills, but his *vision* of the game, his awareness. The first couple of steps make all the difference.

Bobby Smith

Why is Beckenbauer so good? He's dangerous because he can pinpoint passes over fifty yards or over five. He *uses* his teammates, always to best advantage. His anticipation is great, he reads the game well, he's a *smart* player. He can make the necessary changes immediately. He likes the space on the field, likes to go to it. He always finds the space. He makes himself felt. Some players "hide" on the field but he doesn't hide at all.

Al Trost

It all boils down to imagination. Know what you're going to do ahead of time—be an artist with the ball.

Greg Villa

THE KICKS

Several different kinds of kicks are required for facile all-around play. Obviously, a short pass to a nearby teammate has little in common with a powerful shot on goal. You need appropriate techniques for the many and varied situations you'll encounter on the field.

Instinct tells us to kick with our toes. That's what a youngster, or anyone unacquainted with soccer, will do upon first trying to kick the ball. But, as we've said, soccer is not a game of "doing what comes naturally." You have to learn unnatural movements to kick properly, and then to make those movements part of a "naturalized" flow of your body.

The toe kick is easiest at first, but ultimately it proves the very worst kind of kick for a soccer player. A toe kick is much more difficult to control than any other kind. When the ball is wet, a toe kick is completely wild and unpredictable. Toe kicks lack the power to overcome strong winds on the field—such kicks usually loft and are carried wherever the breezes happen to blow. When you need a light and accurate touch or hard-driving, goal-scoring power, the toe kick will not give it to you. Worse, soccer shoes don't protect your toes, and you risk fracturing small toe bones if your toe makes anything less than direct contact. Simply put, *you should ban toe kicking from your game altogether.*

Kicking the ball in soccer is, quite literally, a snap. A snap of the *knee* muscles, not the leg. You should, in general, avoid large sweeping swings of your leg when kicking a soccer ball. Using your whole leg throws you off balance, diminishes your accuracy and your concentration on the ball, and does *not* add significant power to your kick. Both power and accuracy are best served by a good snap from the knee muscles (the lower thigh). When you snap from the knee, rather than using your whole leg and hip, you can also get your kicks off much quicker. That's of utmost importance in every aspect of the game, from a short pass to a sudden nailing of the goalie for a score.

For passing you'll generally use the side of your foot. For shooting and long passes use the classic soccer-style kick, the *instep* kick.

The Instep Kick

The instep, for the purposes of soccer players,

runs from the ankle to the beginning of the toes on the *top* and *inner side* of each foot.

Most beginning players have trouble kicking on the laces with the toes pointed down—coming straight on the ball that way often results in stubbed toes or in kicking the ball too close to the toes for sufficient power and accuracy. The solution is to point your toes slightly outward and approach the ball at an angle, in the classic soccer style. Later, after you've mastered an angled approach, you can learn to come to the ball straight on.

With your foot pointed down and out and your body leaning toward the direction of your kick, you actually meet the ball with a foot that is curved to match the curve of the ball. Contact is made on the laces (tilted down) or on a line stretching from the top of the ankle to the base of the big toe.

A great deal of your foot is in contact with the ball this way. Your accuracy and power are improved in direct proportion to the "amount of foot" that meets the ball. You wrap around the ball as you smack it. The impact flattens the ball against your foot momentarily; then the ball springs away. (You'd need a slow-motion photo to see this.)

It's important to swing at the ball from your knee. Avoid the ungainly windmill swinging of an entire leg pivoting at your hip. Try to keep the hip uninvolved. Watch some beginning players. Watch what happens when they kick the ball and miss. You'll see that missed kicks are almost always the result of a big, straining kick from the hip.

1. Keep your eye on the ball at all times.
2. Approach in a smooth running stride. Don't rush in a panic to connect.
3. Lean forward as you approach.
4. Place your nonkicking foot a comfortable distance alongside the ball. (You'll have to get used to the exact placement through trial and error in practice, but if your kick is giving you problems, your nonkicking foot is probably too far forward or back.)
5. Kick *through* the ball. Let your foot follow through on the kick. Don't get in the habit of stopping your foot as it hits the ball. A good follow-through can have an almost miracu-

An instep kick on the run. See how the kicker's nonkicking foot is planted close to the ball, and how his kicking foot is ready to snap from the knee, his eye concentrating on the ball. At the moment of impact, the kicker's weight will be forward and the kick will be low and powerful.

lous effect in terms of increased power and accuracy. (There are times when you'll want to limit your follow-through, as we'll see later, but this is only for special effects.)
6. Keep your arms out for balance.

Using the Instep Kick

The instep kick has a number of variations and applications. An infinite number of situations can arise on the soccer field—you've got to know all of the available techniques if you want to deal with every possible eventuality. One measure of any player's ability is how quickly and accurately he can kick under any circumstance that arises. So you should know not only how to kick with your instep, but how to make the ball do what's needed when you're using the instep kick.

With your instep, you can create a ball that stays on the ground, one that stays low and bounces, one that travels hard at waist height, one that flies high and rising, one that floats just over the opponent's head, one that spins and curves, one that overshoots your teammate, or one that drops elegantly right at your team-mate's feet.

The ball is eight inches in diameter, but only four of those eight inches are useful to the player who wants to kick the ball off the ground. If you meet the ball at a point high above the middle, it will just stay on the ground, like a dubbed golf shot, and your feet will slide over it. If you meet the ball at its lowest point, it will travel high and not very far. But if you kick the ball about two inches below the middle, it will gradually *rise* in a straight line, and from a distance of about thirty-five feet it can end up in the upper corner of the opponent's goal.

If the ball is kicked in the center, it will move well but stay at ground level. This makes goalkeepers very nervous. Balls at ground level travel faster, and they have a habit of bouncing off opponents' or teammates' legs and into the goal. Too, it takes longer for a goalie to dive down for a ground ball. On attack you'll have more team control and more potent shots if you keep the ball on the ground.

Lofting the Ball

When you need to kick long distances—hitting a wing running downfield or clearing the ball on defense—you must loft the ball, get it off the ground, for the ground slows it down. Your basic point of contact is *just below the center line on the ball*. Although you'll have to concentrate on getting under the ball and bringing it up, try to avoid catching the ball too low, or you'll lose power and accuracy (as in the toe kick).

1. Approach the ball from an angle so that your foot can be turned a bit sideways to the ball. That helps you place the contact in the lower hemisphere.
2. As you come up to the ball, your *nonkicking* foot should be placed one-half to one foot to the side of the ball and slightly *behind* it. This helps your kicking foot come "up from under" on the ball.
3. In lofting, *unlike other kicks*, you can lean

Pele, his arms out for balance, shows us the perfect follow-through form for an instep kick. Practice your form, and effective kicks will follow.

your body slightly backward just as you are about to kick the ball. Your foot will then follow through the ball in an *upward* direction. When you follow through upward in this way, the ball will tend to go upward too.

4. Be sure to follow through with your kick to get full power. Your leg will be outstretched, your toes pointing upward.

5. Just because you're trying to kick the ball in a rising trajectory, don't at the same time look up in the direction that you intend the ball to go. Avoid this common mistake. *Always keep your eye on the ball when you are kicking.* You should *see* the contact when your foot hits the ball.

Low Drives

Nearly all of the special techniques required to kick the lofted ball are reversed when you want to keep the ball low. In general, the low ball is much more valuable in soccer than the lofted ball. Low balls are much more controllable, both for the kicker and for the receiver.

The low-driving instep kick is used for sharp, medium-range passes to a free teammate, and it is the kick generally used in scoring goals. Many beginners simply use an instep kick to shoot on goal, but shots on goal should almost always employ the low-driving instep technique. Nothing is more frustrating than the clear shot that goes soaring up over the crossbar. And this is an eminently preventable mistake.

To keep the ball low your foot should make contact with the ball *right in the middle*, not slightly underneath as with the lofted ball. (To keep the ball on the ground you make contact slightly *above* the middle.) Focus your energies right on the midpoint of the ball, right at the equator. Always keep your eye right on the point at which you want to kick the ball—your foot will tend to follow your eye. In many ways a strong will is as important as powerful calf muscles.

When you approach for the kick, place your nonkicking foot *alongside* the ball, not slightly behind it, as with the lofted kick. This way your knee will be right over the ball at impact, ensur-

Down-pointing toe and follow-through keep the ball from lofting too much. The kicker is still watching the point on his foot where he saw the ball make contact—even though the kick was taken from the eighteen-yard line and was an attempted shot.

ing that your foot does not sneak underneath the ball.

Lean your body forward. The forward motion of your body weight actually supplies the power for this kick, much more so than any force in your leg. Again, at the moment of impact your knee will be directly over, even in front of, the ball. Obviously, you kick *from the knee*, not with a big swing of the hips.

Point your toes down as sharply as possible so that *the middle of your instep* impacts *the middle of the ball,* like a hammer hitting a nail dead-on. As the kick is made, snap forward from your knee and follow straight through. The follow-through will determine the direction of your ball. Point your toes down on the follow-through—that further ensures against any tendencies you might have to get under the ball and loft it.

Stay *over* the ball when you kick a low drive, not behind it or ahead of it. Keep your thigh and knee pointing straight down onto the ball. Keep your *head* slightly forward, and your body weight will follow through by itself.

By all means, master the low-driving instep kick. You can get by in soccer without some techniques—such as the lofted kick—but nothing is more important to your game than an accurate and powerful quickly executed low instep kick.

This is the kick that opens up the field as a pass to your wing or free striker. This is the kick a defense player can use to clear the ball from dangerous zones. And this is the kick that scores goals.

Chipping

Sometimes a defender blocks your path for both dribbling and passing. You can't get around him, and you can't, to be sure, go through him. The only way for you to move the ball to your teammates, then, is to go *over* the defender. For this maneuver you'll use a third type of instep kick, the *chip*.

When you chip, the idea is to make the ball rise steeply up and over the opponent's head. You're not worried about power and distance here, just about getting the ball "up and over." Chips are especially effective when you're at-

tacking near the opponent's goal. You chip across to your striker, over the heads of the defending fullbacks and to the open side of the goal. Your striker takes your chip and heads it or kicks it into the nets with no one in front of him to interfere.

The kicking action for the chip is similar to that for the lofted instep kick. Here, though, your toes are not pointed down. Your heel is kept down so that your foot is horizontal, parallel to the ground. You are using your foot in the manner of a golf club—as an iron to lift the ball out of the rough. The main idea is to get your foot down under the ball. Aim for the part where the ball touches the ground.

At the moment of contact, bend your toes upward, lean your body markedly backward, and scoop the ball up with your instep. You're using your foot almost like a hand—down, under, up with a scoop, and kick with a snap from your knee. If you do it right, your ball will fly up high and have plenty of backspin. (This keeps it from skidding past your target.) Snap down from the knee, scoop up when you make contact. It's a kind of chopping motion.

The chip is useful in many situations. You can even chip over a defender and run around him to continue a dribbling play. But it's a technique that requires plenty of practice before you can control it well. Practice against a wall at first, chipping balls that are coming toward you—those are the easiest chip shots. Then move on to the more difficult ones—the chip shots that are made when the ball is moving away from you or when it's stationary. Practice putting a good backspin on the ball so that it doesn't "run away" from your teammate when it lands.

The Side-of-the-Foot Kick

This kick is sometimes used for shooting or longer passes, but usually the *side-of-the-foot kick is the basic staple for short passes*. It's the most accurate and controllable of all soccer kicks. And it's the easiest for your teammates to receive, too, because the ball stays close to or on the ground. If you had to play soccer with only one kick, this would be it. Actually, don't even think of it as a kick. Think of it as the basic passing technique.

Think, now, of the side of your foot as a golf putter or a croquet mallet. Turn your toes completely outward, and lock your ankle. This "out-footed" position feels awkward to many beginners, and they resist learning it. The side-of-the-foot pass, though, is one of those unnatural movements that you must incorporate into your body and "make natural" in order to be successful at soccer.

By turning your foot outward, you expose the most possible foot to the surface of the ball. This is what gives you control. A slight change in the angle of impact will send the ball with the greatest accuracy in the direction you choose to send it. Your foot twists out, your knee twists out, and your hip twists out. Your leg becomes a new thing. It's more like a swinging mallet than a kicking limb. As soon as you become accustomed to this kick you'll see the whole world of soccer open up to you.

Place your nonkicking foot about six inches from the ball (its toes are usually, but not always, pointed in the direction you want the kick to go). Swing your leg in an easy motion straight through the ball, making contact with the ball with the broadside solid part of your foot just below the ankle. Hit the ball right at its midpoint.

Keep your head down, your eye on the ball always. Follow through after you strike the ball. Keep your arms out for balance.

There's more to the pass than simply kicking the ball smoothly with the side of the foot. In order to time your passes properly and to avoid mis-kicks and mistakes, you've got to play the ball in a light and lively way, as opposed to the heavy and deadly manner of most lazy or timid players.

You can't just stroll up and bat the ball with the side of your foot like an elephant. The only way you can get proper position behind the ball for your pass is to be light, up on your toes, your weight forward, doing a little dance. Sometimes you need a broad step up to the ball to pass it right, sometimes you need a quick hop. Bounce a little, be alert.

This pass should be on the ground. That's where your teammates can handle it best. To keep the ball on the ground, keep your head down, lean over the ball (your weight forward),

and place your nonkicking foot right on line with the ball, not behind it. If your side-of-the-foot passes begin to loft, you're probably leaning backward. Remember (and this would not be repeated so often if it were not so important), up on your toes, weight forward, always alert and dancing. The moment you sink back on your heels, gravity takes control of you—and it takes you twice as long to act.

The side-of-the-foot pass uses a turned-out foot like a golf club or a croquet mallet. Note that the knee of the nonkicking foot points in the direction of the intended receiver.

The Outside-of-the-Foot Kick

You can't always be in the right position to kick a ball with your instep or the inside of your foot. And sometimes you don't want to be. You can use the outside of your foot to quickly flip a ball off to the side or to give a ball outside spin (to make it curve outward). Defenders are often surprised by the outside-of-the-foot pass, since most players generally use some form of instep kick. Although the outside-of-the-foot kick often lacks power, if you point your toes down and in, you can make contact at your "outstep" and put great force behind the ball.

For an outside-of-the-foot pass, point your toes down and in, and lock your ankle so that your foot serves as a mallet head. Strike the ball with a good snap from your knee. Depending on the natural curve of your ankle, you'll find that the ball has a tendency to spin away in an exaggerated way. Practice against a wall until you discover just where to make contact with the ball to achieve an accurate kick. Since this kick is not a particularly powerful one, your follow-through is especially important.

"Bending" the Ball

In the course of play you will often need to kick a ball that curves, that "bends." Sometimes you won't be able to pass directly to your teammate because an opponent partially blocks the line of flight. Sometimes you will need to lead your teammate in a certain direction with a curving ball. And Pele has shown us many times how vicious a curving shot on goal can be. Bending, spinning shots are extremely difficult for a goaltender to judge—even if he can get to them, the extra spin or arc may be just enough to help the ball skid off his hands and into the net.

Bending the ball is not hard once you've mastered the instep and outstep kicks. Kicking right-footed, you get a good spin to the left by hooking down and around the ball, dropping your weight slightly to the left. Imagine that the ball is divided into vertical thirds. By contacting the ball at the outside third, you'll turn it left. And the opposite is true if you want to turn the ball right. Using your *outstep*, you can turn it to the right by contacting the inside third.

Let's say that your right wing is open and that there's also an open space between him and the goal. Intead of passing directly to him, you kick in his direction, but you also spin the ball to the left. This puts the ball in front of your right wing, but it's also angling toward the goal. As

Here the outside-of-the-foot pass is the only possibility. Note that the passer's knee is right over the ball. This pass will stay low and on the ground.

the right wing comes to receive the ball he is now in perfect position for a cross pass or a shot.

The bend keeps the ball in fast action. Your teammate won't have to stop and trap the ball—he can move right into it. The bent *shot* is also a favorite of professional players.

Fig. 1

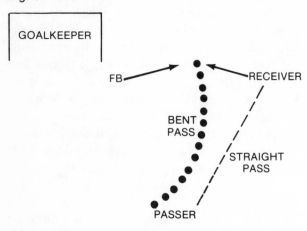

Fig. 2

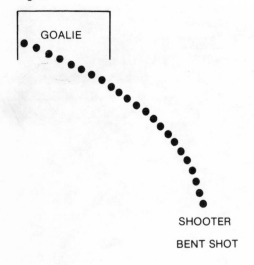

SHOOTER

BENT SHOT

Backheeling

Your opponent expects some kind of conventional technique when you are in possession of the ball, whether it be an instep kick, an outstep kick, a side-of-the-foot pass, or a dribble. Since the defender expects the ordinary repertoire of movements, he will position himself accordingly. He will guard against propulsion of the ball to the left or the right, but rarely to the rear. However, if your defender is close to you, the rear may be the only space available.

Kicking with the heel is a sophisticated and difficult technique, but the effectiveness of the technique is enhanced by the fact that a heel kick is almost always unexpected. A heel kick takes the defenders by surprise. Suddenly the ball is where they had not expected it to be, and this can totally change the direction of play. The deceptiveness of the heel kick is what makes it so valuable.

The heel bone is narrow, so a great deal of practice is necessary before you can make a soccer ball do what you want with the heel kick. Accuracy of contact is crucial.

You need to have your weight well off the ground for backheeling because the motion is fundamentally unnatural and awkward. If you want to backheel with your right foot, take a short hop past the ball on your left foot. Swing your right foot over the ball, and then let it swing back like a pendulum.

You can feint by stepping in front of and across the ball with your left foot, as if to dribble right, and then quickly backheel so that the ball winds up going left instead of right.

Remember, you have to get in front of the ball in order to backheel it, so avoid trying this technique in the middle of a fast-moving dribble.

Fig. 3

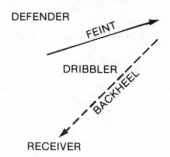

You can use your heel to great advantage in picking up a pass, in the air or bouncing, that falls short of you. Let's say that you're heading down the wing space and that your teammate has dropped a pass just behind you. Instead of stopping and running around behind the ball, try to hook under it with your heel and to flip it up over your head so that it lands in front of you. This is a great time-saver, and it will usually throw the defender off guard since, again, he will not be expecting your maneuver.

Sending the ball backward is almost always a surprise, but before you use this maneuver, be sure that a defender isn't waiting for the ball along with your teammate.

Obviously, this is a hard one. But it is skills such as being able to pick up a short pass and to convert it into a good leading pass that distinguish the outstanding player from the ordinary player.

VOLLEYS

In soccer, unfortunately, the ball never seems to come to us just as we'd like it to. There's never enough time, it seems, to get the best possible position on the ball. Nor, in this fast-moving game, can we often afford to slow the ball down and relieve the tension of peak performance.

Soccer's a game of instinct or instantaneous thought, not a game in which you can take the time to "stop and think." Stopping the ball often leaves you vulnerable to theft or block by the defenders. If you watch truly great soccer players and teams, you'll see that they often use a "one-touch" style. When the ball comes to a player, "one touch" and it's gone again.

The volley is used to "one-touch" the ball when it comes to you in the air and there is no time to trap it. When trapping would lose the vital jump that you have or could get on a defender, you volley. And volleying is virtually a necessity for any player intent upon the win-or-lose aspect of soccer—scoring goals.

The keys to good volleying are timing, alertness, and concentration. The need for power in the volley kick is minimal. In fact, the most common mistake of beginners who are learning to volley is that they try to put too much power into the ball. The ball is already moving in relatively friction-free air. It has power of its own. A short touch on a volley goes a long way.

Remember, to volley well, to kick the ball in midair and send it where you want it to go, concentration is crucial. You should always be able to see the ball make contact with your foot. You must be light on your feet to get the right position and balance when meeting the ball. Remember also that every alteration in ball contact and weight distribution is exaggerated in a volley. If you tend to loft a ball on your instep kick, you're likely to send it sky-high on a volley. Pay special attention to the techniques here—sloppy skills become lighted in neon when you volley.

The Side-Foot Volley

If a ball is low enough, you can volley it with the side of your foot, just as in the side-of-the-foot pass. The side of your foot is best for volleying because its broader surface area lessens the chances of missing or mis-kicking the ball. Volleys are not easy to control—it's best to work toward accuracy rather than sheer power.

When the ball comes to you (up to about lower thigh height for this volley), don't *kick* at it. Get the side of your foot firmly planted behind the ball, and just give the ball a little punch. The ball will have a surprising velocity of its own, as we've mentioned. Remember to be up on the toes of the nonkicking foot, with your arms out for balance. Balls in the air are hard to judge. You'll have to make split-second adjustments when volleying, and that will be impossible if you're not light and bouncy on your feet.

If you want to volley the ball to a teammate for a short pass, as the ball hits your foot, let the foot rebound slightly, like a cushion, to deaden the flight of the ball. Be sure to raise your leg up high enough to make a good square impact with the ball. Tilt the foot upward if you want to pop the ball over a defender's head, or downward if you want to lay a pass at your teammate's feet.

The Instep Volley

When the ball is low and you want *power*, you do not volley with the side of your foot but with your instep. The instep volley is typically used for shooting goals.

Here again, timing and concentration are the keys. Meeting the ball, just as with batting in baseball, is far more important than a big swing of your leg.

To maintain accuracy in an instep volley you must *point your toes down*, lock your ankle, and impact the ball directly on your instep.

Don't kick with your leg—use a quick snap from your knee. But even the knee snap is far less important than meeting the ball accurately. Keep your follow-through to a minimum, because a big follow-through will often result in lofting. *Controlled impact* is the secret of the volley.

As with the normal instep kick, keep your head down, your eye on the ball, and your weight forward. At the moment of contact your knee should be directly over the ball.

When the ball comes in high—at or above knee level—you can't simply meet it with your instep. If the ball is high, your knee will be below it, your instep will come up underneath it, and you'll hit the soccer equivalent of a pop fly.

In such cases you have to position yourself *sideways to the ball*, bringing your instep around behind it, your knee on the side of the ball. Think of your leg as a tennis racquet or a baseball bat. Here your body will be leaning *away* from the ball so that your leg is free to swing sideways.

The Long-Ball Volley

Sometimes it is necessary to get off a long kick from a volley. This is particularly true for defenders, who must occasionally boot the ball downfield to get it away from their own goal.

The long-ball volley is also an instep kick, but here you're aiming for distance and power, at the expense, perhaps, of some control. Kick as you would for the instep volley low ball, but this time *lean back* slightly from the ball. This will get your instep underneath for loft. You should be planted on the ground in such a way as to be considerably behind the ball when you actually kick.

Since this kick is for power, try for a much greater swing of the leg than with the other volleys. Now you want to actually kick from the thigh. And follow through completely—send your energy all the way through the ball and to your destination.

The Overhead Volley, or Bicycle Kick

The overhead is surely the most spectacular play in all of soccer. It's not particularly useful for all

Pele demonstrates perfect lofted volley form for a crowd of onlookers (above).

In this high-ball volley, notice the bent knee which enables the instep to reach up to the height of the ball. The closer the player is to the ball, the more the knee must bend. Notice also the player's intense concentration. The onrushing tackler is totally ignored (below).

but the very best players—because this kick is so hard to master. But there's only one way to learn difficult skills: try them. The overhead is positively thrilling once you learn how to do it, and at most levels of play your opponents will be momentarily stunned by your use of this technique.

In the overhead, or bicycle, volley, you kick the ball backward, over your ducking head, with a scissors motion. The higher the ball *when you make contact*, the lower the flight of the ball off your foot. You want to reach up as high as possible to make your kick, so that the ball will fly straight and true behind you (that is, straight into the opposing goal).

It's possible to simply raise up one leg and make the kick, but the best way is to use a scissors motion and really throw yourself into the technique. This flamboyant, acrobatic maneuver is most successful when it is performed fearlessly and with total enthusiasm. You'll wind up on the ground when you're finished—if you haven't been holding back.

The ball is sailing through the air, floating over your head and past you. If you are going to kick it right-footed, you raise your *left* leg first. Then you swing your right leg up in a fast scissors motion, making contact with the ball above your head. You fall as you kick, so that your head and upper body automatically remove themselves from the path of the ball.

Falling is the element that scares off most players. If you practice a little you'll see that the fear of landing on your head or otherwise injuring yourself is really quite unfounded. Practice kicking your legs up in the air and falling backward, bracing your fall with your hands. Once you learn that you can fall without hurting yourself you'll see that the bicycle kick is not really so hard. Fear is a much greater hurdle here than lack of athletic ability. Lean backward as you kick—*intend* to fall.

TIPS FROM THE STARS: THE GREAT PLAYER

The great player has confidence, ability, desire, and dedication and is a hard worker who is willing to sacrifice. The reason Pele is so great is not because he is particularly fancy, but because he does the *basics* better—the push pass, the trap, the chip pass. The key to Pele's greatness is *consistency, consistency under pressure.*

Alan Mayer and Arnold Mausser

Your mind is the key—knowledge of the game and concentration are more important than physical attributes.

Greg Villa

Volley Practice

An excellent way to practice all of the volleys is to rig up a soccer ball on a string. Then you can learn exactly how much stretch and what kinds of balance are required at various ball heights. Hang the ball from a tree limb, perhaps wrapping it in some netting to make it easier to set up. (You can even use a tennis ball or a soft object if you're unable to rig up your soccer ball.) Practice the bicycle kick on this hanging ball too, until one day you're ready to reveal your newly developed flash in a surprise moment on the field.

Review of the Kicks

As we've seen, a soccer player has a repertoire of kicks to handle various situations, just as a tennis player has a repertoire of strokes. If you are new to the game, these varieties of experience can seem overwhelming, but they're really quite simple. Look at the accompanying chart for a review of the kinds and uses of kicks, and some key points to keep in mind for each kick.

Kicking Principles

The act of kicking is governed by certain principles. If you are having trouble with your kicks, try to analyze what you are doing wrong (and right!) by applying the *basic principles of kicking* to your technique.

1. Kicking is a controlled act. There's almost never a situation in soccer where a big swing from the hips is appropriate. Kick with a snap of the knee, adding a powerful thigh

action only for long balls (which are rarely used).

2. You must keep your head down and your eye on the ball—right to the point of impact—for all kicks.
3. The placement of your *nonkicking* foot determines the flight of the ball:
   a. Behind the ball for a lofted ball.
   b. Alongside or slightly in front of the ball for a low kick.
   c. Near the ball for an inside spin.
   d. Away from the ball for an outside spin.
4. Weight forward for a powerful low drive, weight backward for a lofted kick.
5. The scale and direction of your follow-through are of great importance in determining the flight of the ball. Many beginners underestimate follow-through, but this factor reflects just how you have kicked the ball in the first place.
6. No toe kicks.
7. Run up to the ball with an easy, normal stride. Without a smooth and properly timed run you can't develop the organic flow of movement that is the essence of soccer.

"Inner Kicking"

So much depends on your attitude toward the ball. As we've said, the ball is space enclosed in leather. It's not a hard object, and it doesn't want to fight you. When approaching any maneuver, you need to be able to say to yourself, "This ball will do what I want it to." Because the skills of soccer take some time to acquire, many beginners don't feel that way at all. They say to themselves, "Oh, oh, that ball is about to outwit me again." Your game will open up tremendously once you realize that a great many mistakes and inabilities result from *fear of the ball.* Remember that it's just a ball, after all, nothing to be afraid of.

Kick	Situation and Use	Points to Remember
Instep	Medium pass, long pass, shooting	Toe down, body forward, knee over ball; kick from knee; meet ball in middle
Lofted instep	Long ball	Approach from side, non-kicking foot *behind* the ball; lean back slightly
Low instep	Low pass, shot	Nonkicking foot alongside the ball, weight forward, toe down
Chipping	Pass *over* defender or goalie out of goal	Contact ball near ground; short, chopping kick
Side of the foot	Passing, some shots	Weight forward, foot broadside to ball, contact in middle
Outside of the foot	Passing, some shots	Turn toe in; follow through; weight forward
Bending the ball	Passing, shooting	Contact ball on outside or inside third; weight off slightly to opposite side
Backheeling	Passing	Step in front of ball first
Side-foot volley	Pass, shot, one-touch ball in air	Meet ball broadside; weight forward, light on toes, usually angle down
Instep volley	Shot, defensive clearance	Avoid kick from hip; accuracy more important than power
High-ball volley	Clearance, shot	Get sideways to ball; contact in middle
Long-ball volley	Clearance, long one-touch pass	Lean back slightly; follow through; contact slightly below middle
Overhead volley	Shot, clearance	Scissors in air overhead; fall afterward, and break fall with arm; contact ball high above head

Concentrate on the ball. Make the ball the focus of your whole consciousness when you are handling it. Think of what you are doing with the ball and of what you are about to do with it. Learn to live on the edge between *what is* and *what will be*. There is a strong element of mind over matter in soccer, and in all sports. Many players ignore that element, but it's there all the same. When you kick, you must believe that your kick will be solid. And you must hold clearly in mind the image of what you're trying to do with the ball and of where you're sending it. Hesitation and confusion destroy your technique. Make your decision, stick to it, and follow through. When you shoot, shoot for a place that you have seen in your mind.

The ball is an extension of your mind. It will go only where you first *imagine* it to go. When you pass to a teammate you communicate with him, you pass your *mind* to him.

TIPS FROM THE STARS: THE MIND ON THE FIELD

In soccer, as in any field, you need to put out a very determined effort to get to the top. You have to learn to ignore distractions, to make sacrifices, to give up things. Above all, you have to be *totally self-disciplined*. You can't take the easy way out, and no one can do it for you but yourself. Always set higher and higher goals for yourself—always put out an extra 10 percent.

Bobby Smith

Soccer requires more concentration than any other sport. Although you're part of a team, you must play as an individual. Many games are decided by those individual battles you encounter on the field.

The knee is over the ball, the weight is forward, the eye is on the ball. In this play at the end of a dribble, the dribbler has drawn three defenders to him, leaving at least two receivers potentially free.

Mentally you have to prepare yourself, convince yourself that you are as good as the other player. If you think you're going to get beaten you will. You have to go out with a winning attitude, knowing you can win your individual duels.

I'm nervous before games even though I don't show it. Every player has a nervous feeling before a match. Do what has to be done. Let yourself get wrapped up in the game. Don't let mistakes get you down. Don't let a bad game get you down. Once the whistle blows you've got to be ready to play.

Al Trost

Concentration is the key—a player has to be up for games. You can't go into a game with your mind on other things. The main reason goals are scored is that there are mental lapses—the brain can't concentrate for more than ten minutes. (Meditation might help some players.) When you lose your concentration you have to *work* to get it back—you have to *bring* yourself back. Concentration has a lot to do with physical shape—being out of shape can cause you to lose your concentration. When you're tired you're worried about just making it through the game, and you're not focused enough on the play.

Greg Villa

RECEIVING THE BALL—TRAPPING AND CONTROL

Control is hard. That's why players who learn absolute control over the ball stand out from the rest. Control is even more important than kicking. A team with total control of the ball hardly even needs a good shooter to win matches. A few quick passes and a side-of-the-foot tap into the goal are all it takes. The modern game of soccer relies on short passes and surefooted reception.

You can't use your hands in soccer, but you can teach your body to "catch" the ball as if the body were one big hand. No matter how hard the ball comes to you, you should be able to stop it and put it in position for the play you want. In controlling the ball, always remember that you are *catching* the ball, not merely *stopping* it.

Like kicking, receiving starts with a basic position that keeps you in readiness and permits you to make split-second adjustments.

You need to be light on your feet, loose, and flexible. Keep your knees slightly bent, hold your hands out for balance, be up on your toes, and keep your body soft. When the ball comes to you, it should be as if it were coming to a mobile feather pillow.

One point for beginners: the ball doesn't hurt you. No one sustains injuries from getting hit by a soccer ball. If you give way when the ball comes, if you *absorb* the ball instead of presenting a barrier to it, you'll never get hurt.

Trapping

The techniques of controlling a soccer ball when it comes to you are called traps. They really ought to be called catches, but the word *catches* is not used because it is too frequently associated with the hands and arms. Catching is what you do, though. You catch the soccer ball with your feet, your thighs, your stomach, your chest, or even your head. Once you conceptualize the trapping maneuver as a *catch*, the rest comes easily.

In order to catch the ball with your body, you must treat the ball *gently*, as if it were a breakable egg. You need a soft, supple, relaxed approach to the ball. You trap the ball in the same way that a spider traps an insect in its web—with subtlety and a flexible giving way. You don't block the ball—you draw back slightly at the instant of impact. You draw back so that the ball won't bounce away.

This drawing back is called *cushioning*. You become a cushion that the ball can sink into rather than a wall that it can bounce off. Just as your hand must give way upon impact when you catch a baseball, your legs or chest must do the same to trap a soccer ball.

You generally cushion the ball to slow it down, not to stop it dead. Though you will sometimes need to stop the ball dead, most often you will want to slow the ball down and give it the desired direction at the same time. If you're out on the wing, for example, and the ball comes to you, you don't want to stop it—you want to slow it, bring it under *control*, and *send* it down the touchline in the direction you want it to go.

Trapping, then, is placing the moving ball under your close control. The best trap is one that makes the ball easy to control *and* at the same time sends it in the direction of your intended play.

You should be able to trap while standing still or while running at full speed. The move must often be made quickly—the slower your trap and the slower you gain control of the ball, the more time your opponent has to come up and challenge you. And to block your play.

In mastering the traps discussed below, remember that in all cases the key to good trapping is to cultivate a "feel" for the ball, a light, tender, gentle feel for it. Trapping is no skill for brutes. The only way to tame the ball is through delicate concentration.

Foot Traps

The Side-of-the-Foot-Trap.   Trapping with the side of the foot is almost the reverse of the side-of-the-foot kick. Just as the side-of-the-foot kick is the most frequently used method of ball propulsion, the side of the foot is also the most common trap. The side-of-the-foot trap gives you the most control over the ball, because the length of the foot (from toe to heel) gives you a great surface expanse with which to contact (receive) the ball.

Your trapping foot is turned sideways so that its length faces the ball squarely. The nontrapping foot is pointed forward—usually toward the incoming ball—and is twelve inches or less from the trapping foot. You don't want to get into a situation where your planted foot is far away from the trapping foot, for this will cause you to lose your mobility and your ability to respond quickly to odd bounces of the ball.

In the side-of-the-foot trap, as in the side-of-the-foot kick, you lean your body slightly forward—*weight forward keeps the ball on the ground,* you will recall. As the ball approaches, you raise your trapping foot *slightly* off the ground. (Bend your knee so that the trapping foot is mobile and supple.)

The height of your trapping foot is crucial. It should be just a few inches off the ground, ready to be raised or lowered, depending upon how the ball comes in. When you kick with the side of your foot, your aim is to meet the ball in its horizontal center, and the same is true when you trap with the side of your foot. If your foot is too high, you risk having the ball roll under it. On the other hand, if your foot is too low, a fast-moving ball will roll right over it.

When trapping a bouncing ball with the side of your foot, you must be careful to angle the ball down to the ground and "kill" it. Can you guess, from the direction in which the outstretched arm of the Cosmos is pointing, which way he is about to go with the ball? Your arms lead. Let them float up from your body and help you along.

Your leg must be relaxed as the ball comes, ready to draw back, to *cushion*. How much cushioning is needed depends, of course, upon the speed of the ball. The faster the ball, the more cushioning you'll need to slow it down and gain control. If the ball is especially fast, you can go out and meet it earlier with your trapping foot, drawing your foot back sharply along with the flight of the ball to slow it down. If the ball is coming in at an average speed, on the other hand, and is moving along the ground, you'll probably need little cushioning. You can try a short, slight downward chop on the ball, imparting backspin and stopping it that way.

You can also trap balls with the *outside* of your foot. Here you turn the foot inward, pointing your toe toward the opposite ankle. But this trapping position is useful only for balls of moderate speed—not for hard and fast balls. It is a difficult position for *cushioning*—your knee and thigh simply lack the flexibility to move backward when held in this way.

If the ball is *bouncing,* whether you use the inside or the outside of your foot to trap it, *lean far forward.* You trap just after the ball bounces and, by leaning forward, you bend your knee so that it is far in front of the trapping foot. Thus you make an enclosed space in which the ball is actually *trapped.* You need to be careful with this maneuver, for your foot is now behind you, and your mind can no longer concentrate fully on it.

Fig. 4

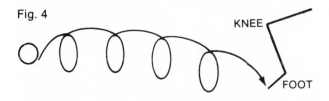

When the ball is bouncing toward you, you must use your leg in conjunction with your foot to smother the inevitable upward bounce. In any trap, you'll have to lean your leg over the ball to ensure successful control.

The Sole-of-the-Foot Trap. This is a dangerous trap, but it can be very effective. Moreover, there are situations where a sole trap is the only controlling possibility—for example, when you lack the split second necessary to get the side of your foot in front of the ball.

There are two ways to execute a sole trap. The first is more a "squeeze" than a trap, and it requires deft timing. Here, as the ball approaches, you simply bring your foot above the top of the ball and come down squarely on it, stopping it dead. The risks of missing or being thrown off balance are obvious.

Another, safer way to trap with the sole is to create a little triangular space in which the ball is literally trapped. In this trap you extend your leg and point your toe upward so that your foot makes about a forty-five-degree angle with the ground. Your foot must come up over the ball and down on it at the moment of impact, or the ball will bounce away. Be sure to have the *rest* of your body directly behind the ball, in case you miss.

Fig. 5

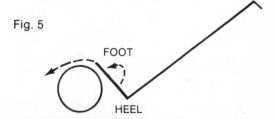

Trapping the high ball means getting way up with your leg and keeping your body behind the ball too. Here the high ball will be knocked down with the sole of the foot—fairly risky, but sometimes there is no room or time for any other play.

The Knee-Shin Trap. This trap is often the first one taught to beginners. It shows very clearly that, yes, you *can* control a strange round object bouncing toward you. And the idea of a trap, of making a little space in which the ball gets caught, is most apparent in the knee-shin technique. Here you control the ball by making a space that it cannot escape from, rather than by slowing its momentum with a cushion.

As the ball comes to you, plant both feet behind the approach point. Bend sharply from the knees and lean forward on your toes. Your legs must be no farther apart than eight inches (the diameter of the ball). You make a triangular space below your knees. The ball enters, bounces against the shins a few times, and dies.

Unfortunately, because the knee-shin trap does not cushion the ball, it lacks reliability. If the ball should take a sudden bounce and hit your knee or the hard bone of your shin rather than get trapped in the triangle, you're going to wind up chasing it. Still, this is a fairly good trap on a rough field with unpredictable bounces, for your whole body stands behind the ball, ready to block it.

Hooking the Ball in the Air. When the ball comes in up high, it is often difficult to trap it with the inside or the outside of the foot, and a knee-shin trap is impossible. High balls can be trapped on your body, as we'll see shortly, or with your instep.

Total concentration is necessary to judge the proper angle for hooking a high ball down from midair. Come up with your leg to the level of the ball. At the point of impact you must *cushion the ball and swing your leg down with a hooking motion at the same time.* Your contact is made at the instep, since this is the only part of your foot that can actually hook around the ball and "grasp" it. You slow the ball by cushioning—giving way as the ball arrives—at the same time you bring it under control by carrying it down to the ground with your foot.

Here, again, a feel for the ball, a light touch, and the utmost concentration are the keys to successful control. In trapping, as in all of soccer, you must never play the ball flat-footed. You must be on your toes, light and bouncy, in

order to make all the necessary last-minute adjustments. Whenever possible, get as much of your body behind the ball as you can. If you misjudge the ball or are surprised by an odd bounce, you'll still have a chance at stopping it. Remember, trapping is not a blocking maneuver—it is an *absorption.*

In England, trapping is often called "killing the ball," and this is an apt expression. When the ball is in motion it is alive. It can bounce and roll far faster than any player can run or react to it. But when you trap the ball, you kill it. You kill its motion, just as you kill the motion of an animal that you have caught in a metal trap. Sometimes you only break the animal's leg; sometimes you actually kill the animal. In either case, the animal is no longer free to go on as it had. Use whatever skills will enable you to kill the ball, as long as you kill it. You must make the ball *your own.*

Trapping on the Body

You can use other parts of your body than the feet for trapping, for "killing." The thighs, the chest, and the head are often the best means for making the kill, and you should master the use of these surfaces as well as the use of your foot. Which part of the body you use depends upon the way in which the ball is approaching, the location of your defenders, where your teammates are positioned, what you intend to do with the ball after you've controlled it, and so on. However, the principles of *cushioning,* a *light and gentle feel for the ball, proper positioning,* and a *relaxed reception* all apply to trapping with other parts of the body just as they apply to trapping with the feet.

The Thigh Trap. When a dropping ball comes to you well below waist height, and you don't want it to drop to the ground, you should use the thigh trap. Your trapping leg should be bent at the knee, so that the foot is facing downward. You "catch" the ball on the *upper part of your thigh.* Don't try to trap down near your knee, because it is extremely difficult to control the ball with the small, hard surface that the knee presents to it. The upper thigh, on the other hand, is soft (keep your muscles relaxed!)

and provides an automatic cushioning effect. Too, should you misjudge the ball, if you use the upper thigh, your body is closer to the ball for a backup.

Raise the trapping leg, and meet the ball with your thigh. If the ball is descending as it approaches you, you should catch it on the top of your thigh and *quickly pull the thigh downward* for a cushioning effect. The ball will bounce a bit, but it should fall relatively dead in front of you.

A ball coming straight at you is harder to handle. In this case you will bend your leg with your foot *behind* you, so that the ball heads toward only the stump of your thigh. At the instant of impact you draw your leg *backward* for the cushioning. You must withdraw the thigh, or the ball will simply bounce right off. If possible, the thigh should be angled downward, aiming the ball to the ground, since this type of ball is much harder to handle than a falling ball. If you aim the ball downward, an excessive but controllable bounce is still at your feet.

The Stomach Trap. The softness of the abdomen and the lower chest makes these parts of the body an excellent cushion for balls that are bouncing up at you from the ground (but beware of taking a sharp line drive in your stomach). When you are moving and trapping a ball in your stomach you can actually carry the ball with you for a few steps—an extra advantage.

To trap with your abdomen, position your body in front of the ball in a mild crouch. *Do not* stick your abdomen out. Rather, tuck it in and make a kind of concave pocket with which to catch the ball. Be sure to keep your arms away when trapping on the abdomen, since there is risk of a hands foul.

Upon impact, if the ball is coming with force, permit yourself to fade backward with a little step or jump. Slow balls will be absorbed by the softness of this part of your body without any additional cushioning.

The Chest Trap. This is an exciting and useful method of killing the ball. As with the

The knees are bent and the body is lowered to enable the ball to land on the soft, cushioning part of the thigh.

thigh trap, the technique varies, depending upon the type of ball you are receiving. The chest presents a large surface for controlling the ball; learn to use it as a cushion, and it will serve you well.

A proper stance will help you to perform the trap smoothly. Stand with one foot in front of the other, your chest expanded and your back slightly arched.

If the ball is coming straight at you, you should *step backward upon impact*. As you step backward, lean forward and allow your chest to cave in. Now your head and chest are arching forward, so that *the chest angles the ball to the ground*. You must aim a horizontal ball downward, for it will bounce away if you meet it straight on, or bounce past you if your chest is angled upward.

If the ball is dropping down toward you, you should arch your back so that you make a kind of table upon which the ball can land. Leaning backward, draw away from the ball as it lands, and you will kill it.

One important way to get good cushioning from your chest is to inhale just before making the chest trap. When the ball hits, quickly exhale. This will collapse your chest and make it soft, creating both a cushion and an entrapment space.

You can use the chest for a deceptive change of direction, because the ball has a tendency to "hang" on your body. Many observers used to say that Pele's chest was covered with some mysterious natural adhesive. There was no adhesive—simply Pele's ability to give way when the ball came to him. To block out a defender or move the ball in a new direction, learn to twist your hips at the point of impact. Twist toward the direction in which you wish to pass. You can then change direction during that moment when the ball "hangs" on your chest.

The Head Trap.   Head traps are extremely difficult. Controlling the ball with the head for the purposes of passing or shooting is tough enough, but killing the ball with the head is a rarefied skill requiring great finesse.

You make contact at the forehead, keeping your neck muscles tight and drawing back and down (to get a cushioning effect) *with the entire upper body*. Your whole torso brings the ball down to the ground, where the life has been taken out of it, and it is under your control.

The chest is arched back, filled with air. Upon impact it is collapsed. When this is done, the ball can roll right down your body and thigh, winding up on the ground before you and fully controllable. Note that the receiver is up on his toes, arms out to avoid a hands foul.

You can trap high balls (left) by making a "table" of your chest. (Right) A chest trap often provides you with an opportunity to carry the ball along your body as you run free from an opponent.

Beyond the Trap: The Transitional Moment

Once you've killed the ball you can't just allow it to piddle around at your feet. A trap is not just a skill for stopping the movement of the ball. A trap is a moment in which you slow the ball down so that you can do something with it. *A trap is a transition.*

It's a *transition* because as soon as you trap the ball you have to make another move. Your move may be a dribble, or a short touch of the ball to clear yourself from a defender, or a quick pass, or a long ball; the move may maintain the direction of the ball or reverse it. In any event, when you trap you should consider yourself as a pivot for the ball, a way station, rather than as a place where the ball terminates its movement.

All of this means that when you trap you should be up on your toes, not flat-footed, that *you should be in motion.* Once you have mastered the basic trapping skills from a standing

position, you must learn to apply these skills on the run. You need to master the constant subtle adjustments that are necessary, because in almost all cases both your body and the ball will be moving. And in almost all cases you will want to *do something* with the ball, beyond merely getting it to die at your feet.

If a defender is directly *behind* you, you should trap the ball so that it moves off to one side (though slowed enough so that you're still in control). If you have a teammate open and nearby, you may transform your trap into a pass simply by not slowing the ball *too much.* If you're a defender you usually will not want to trap the ball dead near your own goal—you will want to set the ball up for your immediate clearance pass.

Sometimes you will trap to best effect if you merely give the ball a little touch to change its direction, hardly altering its speed at all, sending it into an open space which is covered by you or your teammate. Sometimes your trap should be a *nontrap*, a fake. You pretend to trap but let the ball go right past you or through your legs—into the path of your waiting teammate.

The main point to remember, however, is that the trap, the reception of the ball, is a transitional moment. *Trapping does not necessarily mean stopping the ball.* So don't get into the seriously mistaken habit of stopping the ball dead before you make your next move.

Trapping Principles

As with kicking, certain principles apply to all traps. If you are having trouble with any of your traps, refer to these basic *principles* to see whether you can locate where you are going wrong.

1. Upon receiving the ball, you should always remain light, never flat-footed, ready to make instantaneous adjustments.
2. The ball must be "cushioned" upon impact, except when you are deflecting it for a surprise move or a one-touch pass. You must "give" when the ball makes contact with your body. Otherwise the ball might as well be hitting a brick wall—it will bounce right away from you.
3. Angle a trap downward, causing the ball to fall under control at your feet. As in kicking, if you lean backward too much, the ball will fly up in the air. In most traps, you *give* backward but *lean* forward, creating a kind of cave over the ball.
4. Traps should be a prelude to a quick new move with the ball. Receiving is a transition.

5. Always focus all of your attention on the ball. You should *see* the ball make contact with your body.
6. Always present the broadest possible surface to the ball.

Kinds of Balls and the Appropriate Traps

There are no hard-and-fast rules in soccer. Whatever *works* best for ball control *is* best. In general, though, you'll find that the kinds of balls listed in the table below are usually trapped most effectively with the techniques indicated.

TIPS FROM THE STARS: THE MIND ON THE FIELD

You must go out there thinking you're going to win the game, you must give 100 percent effort so that when you come off your conscience is clear. Go with a mind that you're going to play well, you do your own part as well as you can. But you can't play every game well. You're bound to have a bad game or a slump. If you're having a bad game, try to do your best all the time anyway; put more effort into helping out your teammates as much as you can.

Giorgio Chinaglia

Attitude is as important as any aspect of the game. When you get into a slump, it's almost always mental—you lose your con-

Kinds of Balls	*Trapping Techniques*
Moderately paced ground balls	Side of foot, sole
Fast-paced ground balls	Side of foot, knee-shin
Bouncing ground balls	Side of foot, knee-shin
Ground balls when you have a teammate nearby	Side of foot, backheel
Low drives	Knee-shin, thigh, side of foot
Medium drives below waist height	Stomach or thigh, hook with instep
High drives above waist height	Chest
Lofted kick high balls	Chest, head rarely, hook with instep
Balls crossing in front of you	Hook with instep, side of foot, thigh, sole of foot rarely
Balls dropping behind you	Backheel, hook with instep

centration. Talk yourself into better play, psych yourself into it. Don't try to excel yourself, don't try to be too good. Get the ball and just push it when you're in a slump—do the *easy* things. That will help you get more confidence. Don't be afraid to tell your teammates that you're in a slump—ask them to be careful with you, to cover for you, to be alert. Half the game is keeping cool, *keeping your soul, your inner self, approving of what you're doing.* Getting angry at yourself doesn't help very much. Stay with the rhythm of the game, and stay calm.

Bobby Smith

HEADING

Heading is one of the most spectacular and most useful skills in soccer. It is a technique that can be employed for trapping, for carrying the ball forward, for passing, for shooting at goal, and for defensive clearance. Beginners are often frightened of heading, but there is nothing to fear if your attitude toward the ball is an aggressive one. When you head you *strike the ball with your head.* *You* hit the ball—the ball does not hit you.

Any ball above waist height is a potential heading candidate. The key to proper, controlled heading is to contact the ball *at your hairline,* near the top of your forehead. This area is hard and yields a high degree of accuracy.

But mere contact is not enough. You must *punch the ball with your head.* You pull your head straight back—don't just let it flop back in an arc; keep your neck muscles taut—like a cobra about to strike. When you are preparing to head you should also bend backward. At the heading moment you snap your whole upper torso and head forward, meeting the ball straight on with a maximum of power.

You should *step* or, preferably, *jump into* the ball at the instant of impact. In this way you are putting not only the snap of your torso and head into your "head punch" but the force of your body weight as well.

Remember, *go into the ball*—don't simply let it bounce on your skull.

In order to be sure that you contact the ball at the top of your forehead *you must keep your eyes open* and focus all of your concentration on the ball until you strike it. You cannot close your eyes at the last moment because that will throw your concentration off. Follow the ball all the way in. See it contact your forehead.

When you jump to head the ball, avoid the temptation to jump directly into it like a torpedo. Jump first, hanging in the air with your back arched and your head cocked back. Then uncoil your power into the ball by snapping forward. Bringing your legs up behind you when you jump will help you learn this important trick of *hanging in the air before heading.*

As with any other skill in soccer, heading is more than just making contact with the ball and sending it flying. When you head, you always head for a purpose. You direct the ball in a certain way—you keep the ball *under control.*

When attempting to head the ball into the opposing goal, you will ordinarily want power and accuracy behind a straight ball. Generally a head shot on goal should be aimed *down,* because it is much harder for a goalkeeper to field a ground ball. This is especially true when his mind is focused on a ball that was high in the air just a moment ago. When the goalkeeper is far out of the goal, however, you can try lofting the ball up over his head and behind him. To do this, simply get your forehead a bit more *under* the ball, rather than directly behind it or slightly over it, as in a normal shot. High heads near the goal run the risk of going over the crossbar, however.

When attempting to pass the ball to your teammate by heading, you will usually want to try to head it *down.* A ball that lands at your teammate's feet will be much easier for him to handle. To get the ball down, you simply contact it *above* its equator. When passing, you should also bear in mind that your heading power must be adjusted to suit the distance of the pass. A sharply headed ball may be too difficult for your teammate to control. Learning to vary the pace of your heads involves finesse. This is an art that only comes with practice.

When heading defensively, try to come up under the ball a bit. The idea in defensive heading is to get both height and distance on the ball. Naturally you should avoid heading a ball high in front of or across your own goal—that's asking for trouble. Aim for the sidelines to guard against having an opposing player pick up your headed ball for a fast shot.

Like many soccer players, you may find that your most problematic situations are those in which you and an opposing player are *both* trying to head the same ball. This dangerous play can result in injuries from head-knocking, no doubt about it. But as in other situations, an aggressive attitude is almost always your best assurance of safety. You will often be competing for a head ball, and you must learn not to back away from the play. Practice in obtaining favorable position is part of the key to success in this play; the other part is overcoming your fear. If you back off from the ball you will lose it for sure. Neither player wants to get hurt—both must play as aggressively as possible while maintaining an awareness of each other's position and of the potential for injury. The best solution to this problem is to practice jumping and to teach yourself judgment and positioning (you can only learn through practice). If it is *impossible* for you to outjump your opponent, back off and try to intercept his head pass. Being close to him will give you an excellent idea of where he wants to send the ball, and you can place yourself in its path at the last instant.

TIPS FROM THE STARS: HEADING

When you go up for a head, know where your teammates are—look around, see who's where, aim the ball, go up *thinking you're going to win the ball,* and then send it to a man you've picked out when you leaped. Two teammates should never go up for the ball together—it's a waste of manpower. One man should break off and get free for a pass or cover the opponents' passing possibilities.

My way of getting heads is to *get up in the air first*. Your opponent can't get over you if you go up first. When you go up, go up with your elbows out (not sticking way out like wings, just out) so that your *oppo-*

nent can't get close to you. Go up and hang in the air—be up there waiting for it.

Bobby Smith

Heading Principles

1. Punch the ball with your head.
2. Contact the ball on your upper forehead.
3. Jump and hang.
4. Arch your back and pull your head back.
5. Uncoil, and strike the ball by snapping your back and head forward in one fluid motion, as if you were a snake attacking its prey.
6. Keep your eyes open at all times, and concentrate completely on the ball. You should see the ball when you hit it.

DRIBBLING

A good soccer player must be able to dribble well, yet the player who dribbles too much will almost surely cause his team to lose. Soccer is a game of passing, always passing. Dribbling is important, and the great dribbler should be allowed to shine, but the dribble should be used only if it is clearly necessary.

Beginners tend to dribble excessively because they do not fully understand the fluid, interrelated, *team* nature of soccer. The great soccer players dribble only when they have to. The passed ball moves two or three times as fast as the dribbled ball, so passing is obviously superior to dribbling if passing is at all feasible.

Dribbling is the ultimate act of ball control, in a way, because opponents are always trying to take the ball away from the dribbler. And *when dribbling is appropriate*, it's a very potent skill, enabling you to draw defenders into your game and to initiate explosive offensive plays. For the most part, however, you should dribble only:

1. To move to a better field position.
2. To set up a play.
3. To slow the ball down and thus allow your teammates to move into open spaces.

When to Dribble

When you should dribble, and how much you should dribble, depends on where the ball is on

(Top) Go up as high as you can, and contact the ball at your hairline. Note that the head is being aimed down to a free teammate—head should always have a purpose (above). Perfect heading position—up first to block out the opponent, back arched, head cocked back, eye concentrating on the ball (below left). Proper positioning on a head ball can be worth many inches of height to a shorter player (below right).

the field and on the configuration of offensive and defensive players.

Defensive players should be very careful about dribbling. In general, defenders should avoid dribbling when the ball is near their own goal—the risk of having opposing players steal the ball for a shot is too great. Sometimes it may be necessary for you to slow the ball down a bit to enable your offensive players to move downfield, but that's perhaps the only (defensive) situation in which a defender's dribbling really serves a good purpose. More games are lost when defenders "play footsie" with the ball in their own territory than in any other way. A fast pass to a midfielder is virtually always a more effective play.

Midfield is probably the most suitable area for dribbling. Here, when trying to set up an attack, a good dribbler can draw one, two, even three opponents to him, thus freeing his teammates to receive a pass and to begin working the ball more quickly. Often at midfield the player with the ball winds up unmarked (unguarded) and can "carry" it upfield while his teammates set up in the most strategic positions. Be on the alert for such situations—it's better to dribble, even for a great distance, than to risk a pass to teammates who are not in good position. Dribbling in midfield, with two or three teammates dribbling and interpassing in a "weave," is also an excellent way to run out the clock and/or demoralize your opponents.

A good dribble should lead up to a good pass. Teams that have trouble scoring once the ball has been worked down to the opposition goal probably have players who are too dribble-prone. Dribbling near the goal is the mark of a team that is not energetic enough to open up for strategic passes. Defenders can move more quickly than a dribbler, since the dribbler is slowed down by the need to control the ball. And defenders, unlike the midfielder, *must* commit themselves at some point to stopping the dribbler. The goal-area dribbler loses the advantages of speed and opportunity that short, sharp passing can create. So avoid dribbles deep in opposition territory. Sometimes a "bit of dribbling" works wonderfully to throw the defenders off balance and open up a shot. But the problematic offensive player is not the one who does a bit of dribbling. The problematic player

is the showboat who imagines himself able to weave around three intense fullbacks and then to blast the ball past a hapless goalie. Don't fall into such illusions. Watch any NASL game. You'll see that goals are always scored off leading passes and crosses, and *never* by a razzle-dazzle dribbler whose ultimate aim is really ego satisfaction—not goals.

Many players instinctively begin to dribble as soon as they get the ball, and they continue to dribble until this becomes impossible. Then they frantically look around for a pass. If this describes you, you need to look into yourself and to ask yourself why you're doing it. This is the *wrong* way to play soccer. Properly played, soccer is a game in which eleven players work together to move the ball upfield. In its best form, dribbling functions as the lead-in to a good pass. That you can dribble around two or three defenders proves absolutely nothing except that the other members of your team probably spend a lot of time pulling up their socks while waiting for you to pass the ball off.

When you do dribble at the appropriate times, though, there are basics, tricks, and techniques to make the dribble happen in just the way you want it to. And there's a psychological factor that is the single most important element.

Keeping It Close

The most basic requirement of dribbling is that you keep the ball under control by *keeping it close to you.* Learn to pat the ball with a light instep touch so that it stays about a foot and a half in front of you no matter how fast or slow you are going. Keeping the ball close is crucial—it's the dribbling skill that most beginners find hardest to learn. If you let the ball roll too far away you leave yourself vulnerable to theft by a defender. You need to maintain a constant awareness both of where the ball is and of where your opponents are. The closer your opponents, the closer you must keep the ball to your feet. Be sure to look up every couple of dribbles to tune in to the defenders.

Faking

When a defender challenges, dribbling becomes altogether different from merely tapping the ball in front of you. You'll have to use all of your wiles and flexibility to outwit the other player, because he is not encumbered by the need to control the ball. He can move faster than you, so you have to use guile and surprise to keep the ball.

The best ways to fake an opponent are with *change of pace* and *body swerves,* or *wrongfooting.* Although your opponent can move faster than you, you have the advantage of knowing where you are going—the advantage of surprise. Move fast, then slow down quickly (you can even stop the ball dead). Then, when the defender has slowed with you, put on another burst of speed. You should gain a step on him this way, and a step is all you need. Keep speeding up and slowing down, in various rhythmic combinations, until you shake him.

Sometimes you can work yourself clear, but only by a hairbreadth, not enough to give you room to work with the ball. Your *unpredictable* style with the ball can be further complicated with fakes, with wrongfooting and body swerves, to gain the full extra step you need. You must perfect your fakes—not just go through the motions—to make them really effective, because most good defenders are trained to *ignore* fakes and to follow only the ball. Still, defenders also have to try to anticipate. *There is a fraction of an instant during which the defender's attempt to anticipate your move and his concentrated suspicion of a fake come into conflict and leave him indecisive. This is the moment you are trying to create.*

Body Swerve. You can use body swerve to fake out an opponent in two major ways. One way is to swing your body weight in one direction, hoping to draw the defender into the fake, then to quickly swing back and continue in your original direction. This method has a one-two rhythm and will work well against an inexperienced defender. You can also make this a one-two-three (or more) fake by faking one way, faking the opposite way, and returning to the direction of your original fake. The second way is to swerve your body one way, to kick the ball *in the opposite direction,* and then to run around behind the defender to retrieve the ball. This is a difficult play that requires considerable practice and speed. The play is generally called

wrongfooting, because you kick the ball with the opposite foot or in the opposite direction from the one that is expected.

Fig. 6

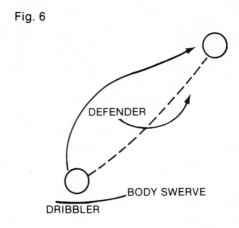

Foot Fakes. Learn to move with small steps behind the ball, so that your opponent never knows on which of those small steps you are going to make your move. Practice feinting a kick one way and pushing the ball off another way—all with one foot while you are hopping on the other foot. You can also fake a forward pass, then roll the ball backward with your heel or sole, giving yourself clear space to the defender's side. One excellent way of gaining that all-important fraction of a second on your opponent is to fake a long kick. You might point to one of your teammates or even call out to him, then swing your leg back as if to kick. When the defender rushes in to block the supposed kick, you have him committed and off balance. Then you simply hook around the ball with your "kicking" foot and dribble away from him, toward the side with the widest angle. You can also stop the "kick," step down with your kicking foot, and pull the ball back to you with your formerly planted foot—thus drawing the defender even deeper into your scheme.

The whole idea is to get the defender moving quickly for the ball. When his ability to stop and turn is thereby diminished, you take the ball into the inevitable opening that he will create.

Fake a pass, fake a kick, fake stopping, fake a burst of speed, fake one or more directions, fake whatever you want, but always pull the defender off his center of gravity.

The Inner Fake. There is a psychological dimension to faking, too. If you are afraid of the defender you will surely lose the ball to him, because it is *your* reflexes that will lag, not his. You must *believe* that you can outwit the defender and get past him. Even if you're not the world's greatest ball handler you must remember that you have the advantage of surprise, that any defender can be faked if you draw him unwittingly into your play. Faking is much more a matter of a cool head than of fancy footwork. If the defender senses that you are scared of him he will move in on you before you have a chance to do anything at all. One excellent fake that you might try—one that most players are too proud to use—is to *pretend* that you are afraid and confused. Then, when the confident opponent rushes in, you will be gone.

Head Fakes. These can work, but they are usually a waste of energy. Any good player will be watching the *ball,* not your head. Foot fakes work because they are within the defender's line of vision as he watches the ball.

The Nothing Fake. If you are playing a cautious defender (this is the most difficult type) who refuses to move in on you, try doing nothing with the ball. Just stand behind it and wait for *him* to make the first move. When he does, go the opposite way. But be sure not to wait too long!

Shielding the Ball

Failure to shield the ball is a common mistake of inexperienced players, but even pros are sometimes humbled by a steal that should never have occurred. Shielding is simple, and once you have integrated it into your game, your ball control will improve immeasurably. Shielding is especially necessary when you are dribbling, but it is also important when you are receiving the ball or picking up a loose ball.

Whenever you are in possession of the ball and a defender is within a threatening distance, you must always try to place your body between the ball and the defender.

If the defender approaches from your left, keep the ball close to you on your right. If the defender is directly in front of you, turn your back to him while keeping the ball close to your feet.

Fig. 7. Shielding.

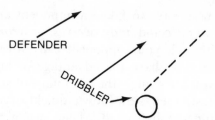

When you shield the ball from an attempted theft in this way, the *opponent cannot get to the ball without fouling you.* You can then keep control of the shielded ball until a teammate moves into an open space to help you out, or you can force your opponent to commit himself and then quickly dribble into the opening that his movement has created.

Keeping yourself between the opponent and the ball seems like a very simple principle, but all too many players overlook this fundamental aspect of controlling the ball while dribbling.

Inner Dribbling: Attacking the Defender

The necessary mind-set when dribbling and when faking are the same. You must carry the ball *aggressively.* You must *attack* the defender when you dribble. You are on offense. You cannot allow your opponent to put *you* on the defensive.

Most players dribble along until they are challenged. Then a voice within says, "Uh-oh, what do I do now?" The defender's presence throws off the flow of the dribbler's movement, and the dribbler shrinks from the conflict. The dribbler *becomes* a defender of sorts now, defending the ball from the defender. When that happens, the defender has done his job, whether or not he takes the ball away from the dribbler.

The *only* way to become a successful dribbler and controller-of-the-ball is to realize that the defender is on the *defense* and that you are on the *offense.* You must attack the defender with your dribble, or you will lose the ball while trying to protect it.

You must fake and feint, make the defender try to guess where you are going and make him guess wrong. You must go into the defender (and then around him) with as much speed and agility as possible. Avoid the common habit of allowing the defender to force you into stopping and slowing the ball down. When a defender comes to you, *attack him.* Go around him, throw him off his stride.

A dribble, when it's necessary, serves more purposes than merely moving the ball through open spaces. A dribble is a way to take one or more defenders out of the play, thus opening up a pass. Or, near the goal, a dribble is a way of creating a scoring opportunity when all of your teammates are guarded. Never forget that the dribble is an *offensive* weapon.

Soccer is a team game, but there is still plenty of room for the outstanding individual play and the effective dribble. As an English coach put it, "Dribbling has become a lost art because we have tended to discourage it. But players who can make themselves something out of nothing close to goal must be influential and must be given license."

Keep a calm head if you want to reach your potential as a dribbler.

THE THROW-IN

When the ball crosses the touchline, the team that was *not* responsible for its going out of bounds receives a throw-in. Inexperienced players often have trouble executing the throw-in in proper legal fashion, but this should not be a problem for players who take the trouble to learn exactly what is required.

Spread your hands out on the ball. You will get the most force on the throw if you try to keep your hands *behind* the ball rather than on the sides of the ball. Your thumbs should almost meet behind the ball.

Now raise the ball up over your head and let it drop behind you. If you let the ball bounce against your spine you will never have to fear committing a foul on this part of the throw-in— most foul throws are due to a failure to drop the ball behind the head before coming up and over the head with it.

You may run up to the line, bouncing the ball or not, but your best power comes from a snap of the wrists and elbows in conjunction with a forward thrust of the upper body, much the same as in heading.

Standing at the line, lean slightly backward as

Pele wrongfoots his defender, faking him right off the field. Now Pele is free and clear to turn back inside. The whole body can be employed for a fake.

In shielding the ball from the defender, keep the ball close and keep your body between the ball and the defender.

Keeping the arms out lightly helps to shield the ball from a would-be thief. With your body guarding the precious ball, no one can get to it.

you raise the ball up over your head and lower it toward your back. Then swing forward in a circular motion with all the snap you can generate from wrists, arms, and body.

Be careful to finish your throw with your head upright and your arms extended in a follow-through. Many players duck their heads as they throw, hoping to gain extra power in this way (and out of fear of hitting the head with the ball). But if you duck your head you cannot throw the ball from *behind* the head, because when the head has been ducked, there *is* no behind to it. The referee will then have to call a foul.

Extending your arms in a follow-through ensures your getting maximum distance and accuracy and at the same time "shows" the referee that you used two hands to throw the ball and that you used them equally.

After the throw, come onto the field quickly and be prepared for a return pass from your teammate. You are unguarded when you throw, and you are often free when you return to the field. We will take up the many possible strategies for effective use of the throw-in during the game situations in our discussion of set plays (see Chapter 7). For now, though, practice throwing a hard, spinless long ball with both feet on the ground. Learn to throw to your teammate's feet or head, behind him or leading him—for the throw-in is a subtle art that can be turned into a potent offensive weapon.

4
The Position

The names of the eleven soccer positions vary according to the style of play, the country in which the game is played, and the strategic alignment that is being used. Generally, though, soccer teams consist of a goalkeeper, defensive players, or midfielders who connect the defense with the offense and play both ways, and strikers or forwards. In this chapter we'll discuss all of the positions, the kind of player best suited to play each (though there are no hard-and-fast rules about that), what the player does on offense and defense, how the position varies according to different styles of play, and how you can make each position rise up and glow compared to the way it's ordinarily played.

Certain features apply to every position, no matter where the ball is and no matter what the level of experience and skill of the players.

All players, in all positions (with the exception of the goalkeeper in some cases), must play optimum soccer. Playing optimum soccer means that you are getting as much as you can from your abilities, that you are coming as close as you can to your potential. To play optimum soccer *every* player should:

1. *Run.* Soccer is a game for runners, not loafers. Whatever your position, you will always make the most of it if you keep running. When your teammate has the ball, run to support him. Run to provide an outlet for a pass, run to an open space. When defenders are guarding you tightly, run to shake them loose. When it's time to shift to defense, you should always *run* back, even if the ball is on the other side of the field and you appear to be out of the play. You never know when a cross, a theft, or a mistake will change things entirely.

When the ball is passed to you, run so that you get to it before your opponent does. Never let yourself get beaten to the ball that you could have picked up with just a bit more hustle. You should always be moving in soccer, always anticipating the play and gaining optimum position. If you're standing around or walking much of the time, waiting for the action to come your way, something is wrong.

2. *Be aware.* Awareness can make you "run faster," because if you are aware, anticipating what will happen (and all the possibilities), you will have an extra jump on your opponents.

Awareness is a way of gaining a head start. And it's the only way to avoid getting tricked or to prevent your opponent from getting behind you. You must always be aware of the location of your opponents and of your teammates. Even before you've gotten the ball, you must know what you will do with it. You need to know whether you have time to set up or whether the opposition is too close for you to do so. What good can you do with the ball if you don't know where to send it? In every situation your awareness of the configuration of play is crucial to your own success and to the success of the team.

3. *Be aggressive.* The hesitant, indecisive, overly cautious, or frightened player is a liability to his team. Aggressiveness means that when you have the ball you fight to keep it, that when a defender tries to take the ball away from you, you "attack" him with your dribble, that when an opponent has the ball, you fight to take it from him and you never let him go. And above all, aggressiveness means coming to meet a pass, anticipating an opponent's pass so that you can intercept it, and *being the first to reach a loose, uncontrolled ball.*

4. *Be in shape.* Later in this book you will find drills for both skills and conditioning. There's nothing more contradictory—and saddening—than a soccer player with his tongue hanging out, too tired to give the game his best. Train yourself for endurance and for bursts of speed off the mark. Otherwise your skills, no matter how good and no matter how conscientiously developed, will be worth nothing.

THE GOALKEEPER

Even if you're not a goalkeeper and you don't want to be one, you should read this section. Every player on the field ought to know something about a goalkeeper's reality. Strikers must know how a keeper thinks, what moves he will make, what are the likely ways to get a jump on him. Defenders must know how he works so that they can support the goalie and know when to expect support *from* him.

Without a good goalie a team might as well not take the field. Even the best defense cannot hope to prevent the other side from taking at least a few reasonably good shots during a game, and if each of those shots gets past an ineffectual keeper, the game is lost, no matter how well the team as a whole may have played. The goalie must have sure hands, of course—he's the only player who is allowed to use his hands—but many other qualities are necessary to play this position well. Quick reflexes are paramount. Shots on goal are kicked *hard.* A keeper must be able to move for them in the hairbreadth of a second. Obviously, a goalie cannot be indecisive either. There are many times when a goalie will have to take possession of the ball right at his opponents' feet. He must be brave as well as sure-handed, alert, and quick.

And there's more. A goalkeeper must be a leader on the field. Since he has the best perspective of any player on his team, he must constantly be telling his teammates where to move, what gaps to fill, whether to let him take the ball or clear it, and so on. And he's a leader on offense, for the goalkeeper's distribution of the ball, carefully considered and executed, should begin a play that can carry the ball all the way down to the opponents' goal. So the keeper must know more than his own role—he has to know the responsibilities of every other player on the field.

What makes a good goalkeeper? All of these qualities—and (as with any other position) much practice.

Goalkeepers should remember one thing above all, because the ball can get awfully slippery even when it seems quite docile. *Always get your body behind the ball.* That way, even if you miss the catch, your body will be there to stop it. Too, you should always try to bring the ball to your chest on the catch, even a ground ball. Clasping the ball to your chest puts it in the safest, most controllable place. A ball that is on the edge between being caught and being missed will be yours if you move to bring it to your chest. Wherever you pick up the ball, bring it to your chest in a graceful rhythmic arc.

You should catch any ball with your fingers, not your palms. The palms are too hard—they create a kind of backboard for powerful shots, causing the ball to merely bounce away (perhaps into the foot of an oncoming forward). When the ball comes to you, spread your hands out behind it and clasp it hard with your outstretched fingers. Cushion the ball, allowing your hands to draw back upon contact, drawing the ball back—hopefully to your chest. Remember, you're not trying to block the ball—you're trying to catch it. On wet days, when the ball is slippery, all goalies should wear goalkeeper's gloves for greater friction and surer grip.

Ground Balls

There are two kinds of ground balls—with a slightly different technique for fielding each.

Hard ground balls require that the goalkeeper go down for them. When bending over from the waist, you simply do not have enough stopping power to be safe. To gather a hard ground ball, go down on one knee. The knee on the ground should point to the ball; the knee in the air should be perpendicular to the path of the ball, to block a potential bounce. In this way your legs are a second line of defense if you should miss with your hands. Your legs make a solid wall which the ball cannot squeeze through.

After you have caught the ball out in front of you, gather it up into your chest with a smooth rolling motion. Come to a standing position as quickly as possible so that you are instantly ready to distribute the ball (throwing it or kicking it), and ready as well to avoid oncoming strikers who may be following up the ball.

You can pick up a *slow-moving* ground ball by bending from the waist. When you do this you should still be careful to get your body behind the ball in case it bounces up. Keep your legs behind the ball, close enough together so that the ball cannot squeeze through them. Though bending from the waist for slow balls is not as safe as going down behind them, it has several advantages. Since you are upright you can move out to the ball and cut it off from any offensive players who might rush in on it. Too, if the ball should hop sideways, you will be able to go for it. Even more important, by remaining upright, you are able to quickly field the ball and send it back to your teammates to begin a new offensive play. The extra time you gain in this way may be just enough to catch your opponents out of position and give your entire team a marked advantage.

High Balls

You have to move out of the goal for a high ball. Catch it as soon as you can—don't wait for it to come to you. If you wait you may be in for a rude surprise as an opponent cuts the ball off and heads it in for a goal. If the ball is a high lob (such as a cross on a corner kick), you'll have to come out and also jump for it, grabbing the ball at the peak of its trajectory. You should be able to reach higher than any player can jump for a head. Positioning can be a problem, though, and it's useful to bend a knee outward when you jump, to protect yourself from the intrusions of other players. Always call out to your defensemen when you jump, so that they know what you are doing.

Diving Saves

When you are forced to dive for a ball—and you should never shirk the dive when it is called for—you must be totally focused on the ball, ignoring other players and your own fears. You must imagine that the ball is a million-dollar bill, yours to keep if you catch it.

You cannot just fall—you must use your legs to thrust yourself toward the ball. Use the leg *on the side to which you are diving* to send you there. If you are going to the right, for example, jump off the right leg. Your whole body must go to the ball with your arms extended outward, as if there were foam rubber below, not hard ground. Reach out for the ball, and grasp it with your fingers. Then curl the ball into your chest. It is all the more important to bring the ball to your chest for this kind of save, for your control is much more precarious when you dive. If you lose the ball while you are on the ground, a goal is virtually assured. You should pull the ball to your chest whether your dive has been on the ground or for a high shot in the air. As a goalkeeper, you must be decisive and bold, and at the same time you should be supercautious. It is better to be careful and nonflamboyant than to fish the ball, frustrated, out of the nets.

Punching and Deflecting

You can't always catch the ball, and when catching is too difficult a play, it's best not to try. In cases where a catch is not feasible, you will

Jump high—you can reach higher with your hands than your opponents can with their heads. Pull the ball to your chest immediately. You're likely to be upended "by accident" in chaotic plays like this. Don't be afraid to dive right over the opposing forwards.

punch or deflect the ball away or past the goal. You will punch or deflect when the ball is too high for you to catch, when you are out of position and can't reach it, when it is coming too fast, or when the ball is high and the goal area is so congested that you might be blocked in trying to catch it.

When you punch, form a fist and punch the ball back where it came from, off to the side, or up and over the goal. The sides are safe, but punching the ball in a new lateral direction is risky because when you punch, it is difficult to control the direction of the ball. Hit the ball *hard*—a weak punch may set up the opposition for a score. Be sure that you are *facing the ball*. That way the timing and accuracy of your punch are greatly improved. Time the jump so that you meet the ball at the peak of your ascent—this is where you have the most power. (Be sure to keep your thumb on the *outside* of your fist, not tucked inside. Otherwise you're liable to wind up with a broken thumb.) One- or two-fisted punching is at your option. Two-

fisted punching is more accurate than one-fisted punching, but it gives you less reach.

If the ball is coming high up near the crossbar, or wide near the goalposts, and there's no way you can reach it with any control, you may want to merely *deflect* it. Deflection involves pushing the ball up higher if it is at the crossbar, or wider if it is near the posts. Deflection is a simple skill, born of necessity, and it is usually a safe maneuver since you use it to send the ball out of bounds. But, *caution,* beware of deflection if you are outside the goalmouth and far from the posts. Deflection is not accurate enough to be a viable technique unless you are right near the goal structure. Nothing is more embarrassing than a goal scored off an ineffective deflection.

Many young goalies who like to play with a lot of style and flash are prone to punch the ball out of the goalmouth when it could have been caught with relatively little trouble. This is a poor way to preserve the sanctity of the goal. A punched ball can never go very far, and you risk having it picked up by the opposition forwards or linkmen. Punching and deflection should be used *only* when the ball cannot be caught. They should never be used merely to demonstrate style and flair.

Positioning and Coming Out

Here is where we separate the true goalkeepers from the ordinary catchers and kickers. The ability to cut off the opponent's shooting angle is a delicate and slowly learned skill, and it ranks as one of the central skills in all of soccer. If you give the opposing striker no room to score, he won't score.

To get a good sense of how, when, and where to come out of the goal and cut off the striker's angle, imagine yourself in the striker's position with a camera. The striker looking through his camera from, say, twenty-five yards out, can take in the entire goal, with you in the middle. As you move toward him, particularly if he is off to one side or the other, you begin to cut off the span of goal that he can see. Finally, when you are close to him, it is as if you have put a hand up in front of the camera lens. The shooter has only a narrow path available if he is to get by you.

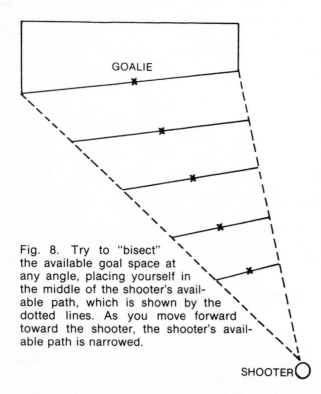

Fig. 8. Try to "bisect" the available goal space at any angle, placing yourself in the middle of the shooter's available path, which is shown by the dotted lines. As you move forward toward the shooter, the shooter's available path is narrowed.

In a breakaway situation, where the attacker is coming on you one-against-one, you *have* to rush out and narrow his available path—otherwise you'll be a sitting duck. And when you do come out, *come out*. If you begin to come out and hesitate, you have merely signaled to the striker where he must move to score. When you leave the goalmouth you *must* capture the ball. Forget the fear that your goal is naked and unattended. You have made your decision, begun your move—now go after the ball single-mindedly and dive for it. Try to narrow the shooter's path and *also* to force him to shoot in a given direction, so that you'll know where the ball's going. You can do this by giving him slightly more goal space on one side. When you know where he must shoot, you get a better chance at corralling the ball. Your basic thrust, though, is to learn how to narrow the shooter's path and to concede as little goal area as possible to the shooter.

Of course, there are risks in leaving the goalmouth, and you have to be aware of those risks when you make your decision to come out. The shooter can chip the ball over your head and into the goal, since there is now space behind you. Such lobs are among the most frustrating of all goals—keep an eye on the shooter, and beware of this possibility. Too, it is very dangerous to come out when there are several attackers near the goal area. If your supposed shooter passes off after you have come out, his teammate may well be looking at an open goal. So be aware of the positioning of all opposing players—including attackers who are *in process,* running toward the goal—before you come out on the ball. When you see a breakaway, be ready to break away from the goal line. If it's two- or three-on-one, go straight for the ball, but be alert for the pass. Knowing when to come out is the great separator of goalies. The best are out often, but not when the risks are too great.

TIPS FROM THE STARS: COMING OUT OF THE GOAL

Going out for the ball is hard—it's so much a matter of judgment. You have to learn how to read the game; you have to

The goalie comes out of the goalmouth to cut off Pele's angle. Knowing that there is now only a limited space in which Pele can shoot, the fullback rushes over to cover the only area open to Pele (above). Although the keeper has been unable to stop Pele's shot, the fullback may well be able to keep the shot out of the goal (below). This play demonstrates both the advantage of coming out of the goal to cut off the shooter's angle and the need for a coordinated, total defense in which every player does what needs doing—always anticipating what might happen.

know where all the players are. You go out to get the ball or to cut off the shooter's angle. A key thing for a goalie is to get the shooter nervous—when the shooter is nervous, under pressure, he can't get off his best shot. On a corner kick, come out when you know you can get the ball. Once you've made your decision you have to stick to it—you can't come out and then stop. When the player against you is a great one, like a Pele, you can't let that upset you. Just see him as another man with two legs. When you come out for a high ball, try to catch it at its peak and at the high point of your jump—nobody can head up over where your hands can reach. Stay compact, and take a leg up with you—knee bent—so that when someone hits you, he's going to hit a leg. You can't *worry* about getting hit—think of the *ball first,* or you'll miss it completely.

Alan Mayer and Arnold Mausser

Handling Crosses and Corner Kicks

One of the most difficult situations for any goalkeeper is having the ball come across the face of the goal. Here the direction of play can change suddenly—the angles from which a shot may be taken are various and unpredictable. Your defenders may be off the ball, and confusion often reigns in front of the goal.

When the ball is crossed in front of the goal, either from a corner kick or from a moving play, do you go for the ball or guard against the apparent angle of shot, which will usually be different from that of the cross? This is always a confusing situation, and unfortunately you have

Fig. 9

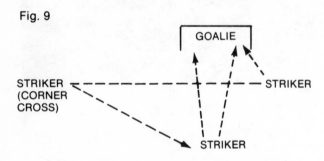

to be prepared for *all* the possibilities. Because the cross is so dangerous, and the new direction that the ball will take is so unpredictable, you should try to *go out and get the ball* whenever you have a chance at reaching it. On high crosses, *always* go up in the air to catch the ball before a striker has an opportunity to head it toward the goal. On low balls, go out and dive on the ball before it reaches your opponent's feet.

If you obviously cannot get the ball, however,

you then tune in to the positioning of the other attackers and move to cut off their angles as soon as it is clear which one will receive the ball. This is a tough play for a goalie, and the best advice is to act positively and decisively. Concentrate completely on the ball so that you do not become swamped by the inevitable confusion created by so many clearly dangerous potentialities.

Wet balls require extra caution and the use of goalie gloves. When the ball is wet, *always* get your body squarely behind it. Take no save for granted. Go all the way down even for very slow balls. The wet ball is an eminently unpredictable beast.

Distribution

What the goalkeeper *does* with the ball after gaining possession of it is as important as any other aspect of his job. The goalie can become a leader on offense as well as defense if he distributes the ball quickly, with good judgment and finesse.

Most young goalkeepers think that once they field the ball they are supposed to give it a good boot downfield. In most cases this is simply a waste of time. The keeper should distribute the ball *to his teammates,* whether by kick or by throw, in the most strategic way possible. The goalie should really be the first player on offense.

Effective distribution means three things:

1. Rapidly assessing the configuration of play.
2. Developing a repertoire of distribution techniques.
3. Maintaining an awareness of the capabilities of your own players.

You must get a fast sense of who is where, and distribute the ball to a player who is not only open but also has support in the form of nearby teammates. Distribute the ball *quickly,* before the opposing team has a chance to set up. Remember, you are passing to a teammate, not giving a punting-for-distance exhibition.

Several different distribution techniques are at your disposal. When you are giving the ball to a free defender on your team, *roll* the ball to

Here the ball is rolled to a fullback with a bowling motion. The ball is kept on the ground so that it is easy to control.

him. In this method (which is good for a short distance because it is accurate, but lacks sufficient power for long distances) you roll the ball *underhand,* as if throwing a bowling ball or pitching a softball. Make sure that the ball rolls smoothly on the ground. That makes it easy for the defender to control the ball—which is the whole point of this method.

If you want to distribute the ball over a longer distance than is possible by rolling, you should throw it from the shoulder. Begin as if to throw a baseball, but throw the soccer ball *sidearm,* roundhouse fashion. If you try to throw overhand, the ball will have too much loft and will slow down in the air. For longer accurate passes you can also place the ball down on the ground and use a side-of-the-foot pass, as would any other player.

Punt when it is necessary to break up the momentum of a pressing attack and when the opposition defenders have moved far upfield and are vulnerable to a fast break by your forwards. Punts are also potent on short fields. But don't merely gather the ball and blast it downfield. Punt *thoughtfully*.

The correct course of action depends partly on who is open and partly on the pace of the game. It also depends on who your players are. If you have a speedy outside striker, for example, a long punt to his side of the field may be appropriate. However, if you have no fast-breaking midfielders, what is the point of booming the ball out to them? On the other hand, if your defenders are not sharp, if they have trouble keeping possession of the ball when challenged, you will do better to kick the ball long. In other words, distribution begins an offensive play, and you should put the ball to your best offensive players whenever you can.

TIPS FROM THE STARS: DISTRIBUTION

Distribution—you get rid of the ball when the opportunity is right, get it out to the wings or the wing fullbacks. *Always switch sides* on your distribution—the opposite side is where you're going to have your free man and fewer opponents. The goalie can control the momentum of the game, and he should. If there is too much pressure, or if your men cannot get free, hold onto the ball for a while. Send the ball to the *outside*—it's safer there, and a mistake or interception in the middle is much more dangerous. Be in constant verbal communication with your men. The goalie should always be the boss because he can see everything—he must take command of the area. Although you should usually try to throw or roll the ball to your teammates, there are times when you should punt: (1) to get the ball down to the other end fast; (2) to give your defenders and yourself a break; (3) when everyone's covered, and there's nothing else to do; (4) against teams that are weak in the air (like the South Americans and the Chinese). But remember, studies have shown that in the NASL you have a 20 percent chance of retaining possession on a punt, as opposed to an 80 percent chance on a throw or a roll.

Alan Mayer and Arnold Mausser

TIPS FROM THE STARS: HOW TO PLAY GOALIE

The key thing for a goalie is to keep himself together both mentally and physically. A field player can make twenty mistakes in a game and not hurt the team too badly, but the goalie *cannot make any mistakes,* since any mistake is a potential goal. You have to be ready mentally throughout the entire game, and this is the hardest part—it's tough to keep your mind from wandering. Always keep tuned to the game—keep telling yourself that the ball is coming down and ask yourself what might possibly happen. Always be anticipating. Tune in to the game, and analyze it even down on the other side of the field, for this keeps you alert, and you might see something that could help your team. Try to play a little game with yourself in which you're a soccer analyst, so that *your mind is always in the game.* If you get caught daydreaming you're going to let a goal through. Psychologically, you have to keep yourself

up, you can't let a bad play get you down. *Confidence is 85 percent of goalkeeping.* Confidence and alertness are every bit as important as ability. The goalie must have only one thing in mind—to get the ball. You can't let yourself worry about anyone else—you do what you have to do. If you go for the ball 100 percent, not held back, and thoughtfully, not wildly, you won't get hurt. Injuries only occur when you lack confidence, when you hesitate, or when you don't give the play your all.

Alan Mayer and Arnold Mausser

One major point regarding distribution of any kind: *never pass the ball to a teammate who is in front of your own goal.* When throwing, kicking, punching, or deflecting, always send the ball *away* from the front of the goal.

Communication

An active goalie who talks to his teammates and helps direct the positioning of everyone on the field can be an immeasurably valuable asset to his team and can make his own job easier at the same time. The silent goalie defeats himself.

If your defenders do not hear you shout for the ball they will be committed to going after it. So if you intend to field the ball you *must* tell your defenders by shouting "Keeper!" If you want *them* to be sure and go after it, shout "Clear it!" or "Defense!" Such communication at the goalmouth is extremely important, because the situation there is often confusing, and defenders are never quite sure what the goalkeeper has in mind. Too, if you shout something like "I've got it!" the *attackers* may well ease off for an instant—just the instant you need to make your play.

Since you have a clear view of the entire game and are not running, you can and should function as a kind of captain or commander in chief. You can send one of your defenders to an unguarded opponent, or bring a defender in to help cover the middle, or even shout up to a wing who is losing advantage by drifting too far toward the center. If your man is challenged, you can let him know where his free passes are, or even call to him to pass the ball back to you.

If you play goalie and you're shy, you have a personality problem to overcome. For your voice must ring out to your teammates, alerting them, advising them, moving them around, encouraging them, providing *leadership*.

THE DEFENDERS (THE FULLBACKS AND THE SWEEPER)

When soccer was less sophisticated, the rule of thumb was to take your two biggest players and make them fullbacks, something like defensive tackles in football. But that was a grievous error. In fact, fullbacks are no longer even strictly defensive players. Beckenbauer, perhaps the greatest soccer player alive, is a defender, yet he scores more than his share of goals and assists. Today, fullbacks should be fast, intelligent, and good ball handlers. They often carry the ball upfield and work with midfielders and wings on offense. The ability to boot the ball the length of the field is no longer particularly relevant or important.

Though the nature of fullback play has changed, fullbacks remain the last line of defense on the field (before the goalie). Fullbacks now play a significant role on offense, but they should never forget that their primary *responsibility* is defensive. Responsibility, in fact, is the watchword of a good fullback. You must never let your opponent get behind you—you must never get "beat." Your responsibility is to slow the ball down, stop its forward or goal-directed progress, and force mistakes from your opponents. Flashy steals and sliding tackles are icing on the cake, not the cake itself. Good fullbacks are often unglamorous and unspectacular, while at the same time they are the most crucial players on the team. Good coaches start by building a strong defense, then work forward. A team that cannot score on you cannot beat you.

As a fullback, you must work on *containment*. The opposition can't be permitted to play its own game or to develop plays with which it is familiar. Containment means three things: slowing or stopping the progress of the player with the ball, cutting off his passing possibilities or actually picking off his pass (a fullback must be a good *anticipator*), and always driving the opposition play to the outside of the field—

where it can do no damage. Taking the ball away from the dribbler should not be uppermost in your mind. If you guard him closely and your teammates guard *his* teammates closely, you will force a mistake that will *give* you the ball. Taking it isn't really necessary.

When coming up on a wing who is driving down the touchline, for example, come up to him at a slight angle so that he can *only* go down the line. Don't give him any room to switch the ball inside. That way you *know* where he will be going, since you have given him only one choice. His maneuverability is less than yours because he must control the ball—so by merely approaching him at the proper angle, you have taken a considerable advantage over him. If he cannot get past you he will have to stop. Your teammates, seeing this, will be able to anticipate and cut off his "escape" pass. That's the way a good defense should work.

Learn to come upon an attacker slowly, refusing to commit yourself until the last possible instant, so that you won't be faked out. Your mission is to *contain* the opponent's play, not to take the ball—that point can't be stressed enough. If you try to move too quickly, if you are too intent on playing the role of hero and stealing the ball, you are liable to wind up watching your opponent taking a hard shot at goal—behind you.

There are certain skills that you should cultivate as a fullback—you will be using them again and again. Your traps must be accurate, controlled, and perfect. A poorly executed trap may give the ball to an opponent with an open field to the goal. Remember, you are the last line of defense. If you make a mistake, there is no one to correct it for you. Your heading must also be excellent. You will often have to stop a wave of attackers with a well-placed head. Learn to judge long, high balls properly; learn to get good power behind them with a good whip from your back; and learn to place your heads to a teammate who can help get the ball started back upfield. The skills described in "Stopping the Ball" (Chapter 6) are also especially relevant to fullback play.

Fullbacks must learn to use the goalkeeper in order to break up offensive plays. Inexperienced players in particular are so focused on keeping

If possible, fullbacks should make it their business to protect the goal area when the goalie must go out.

the ball away from the goal that they don't use the keeper nearly enough. Whenever you're in a tight spot, think of the keeper—look and see whether you have a pass to him. (This includes situations in which you are throwing the ball in from the sidelines.) If you do, pass the ball hard enough to avoid interception by an opposing forward, but be careful not to kick it too hard! The goalie must be able to handle your ball easily. It's a good idea to kick the ball slightly off to one side or the other of the goal, so that even if the keeper should miss (the ball can always take a bad bounce, for example), the worst that can happen is a corner kick. Be especially careful kicking back to the keeper on wet days, when the ball is heavy, slippery, and hard to handle. Bearing these warnings in mind, try to use your goalie whenever feasible. He can break up a pressured attack, and he can often throw the ball off to a free teammate whom you cannot reach or perhaps cannot even see.

When the opposing offense is working the ball in your territory, you must divide your attention between where the ball *is* and where it *might* go. You must mark your opponent, of course, and you must also be aware of the open spaces in your area that a forward might run into. This awareness translates into anticipation. Always watch the player with the ball to see where he is going to pass. If you do, you'll be able to intercept a great number of balls and to turn your team from a defensive stance to an offensive one.

Another part of your necessary awareness is to find out as much as possible as soon as you can about the player you are marking. Find out how he likes to work. Does he always try to make a break down the line, or does he like to take the ball inside? Does he work with another player to create two-on-one situations? Which is his strong foot? Does he try for speedy or methodical movement with the ball? Is the opposing team likely to cross the ball into your territory? Does the opposing team tend to play on one or the other side of the field? (If so, you can move toward that side to help out without creating a dangerous situation.) Get a good sense of how your codefenders are making out. If they are having trouble and you are not, it may be best to move over and help them, even though this means that you leave your opponent less closely marked. In sum, a good fullback must *think* constantly. It is not enough to merely position yourself alongside an opposing player and wait for the action to come to you.

Today, fullbacks are an integral part of the total team offense. Many teams are at their most vulnerable just when they have lost the ball (to a fullback). You should know the instant you take control just how and where you are going to distribute the ball. Know where your forward players are, and where the opposing defense is positioned. Your pass should always be to a clear teammate, to a teammate who can keep possession and start a play—not simply to another player who wears a shirt with the same color as yours.

When the time is right, you can move upfield on offense. Perhaps you have taken the ball and there is no opposition in front of you. Then you can carry the ball downfield untouched, much as a guard in basketball will dribble the ball toward the basket. Often there will be only one or two defenders on your side of the field. If you pass up to your wing or your halfback and you *follow up that pass* by running up to become part of the offensive play, you have become an extra player, an extra advantage, for the offensive move. In a bolt-type offense, this new kind of fullback play can be very effective. But you can't do it in a vacuum. It must be a part of your team's style of play. Your teammates must know that you might make such a move, so that they can cover for you. Too, it's a dangerous play unless it is clear that your team can maintain possession of the ball for the duration of a drive toward the opposing goal.

Except on the occasions when a fullback moves upfield for good reason or moves to help out his codefenders, also for some sound reason, it is extremely important for a fullback to maintain his position, to maintain the sanctity of his territory. If you cross the field, who will be there to cover your area if the ball is crossed back over? You can go, but make sure that someone is covering for you. Your codefenders

expect you to be in a certain place, and so does your goalie. And they play with that in mind. This also holds true for your midfielders and your wings. If they are trapped with the ball and want to backheel it to you, *you've got to be there*.

Wing fullbacks should stay *right on the wings* unless no one is there for them to guard. Sweepers, the middle fullbacks, should avoid straying too far from the middle since that is the most vulnerable area on the field. Too, sweepers should never engage in the kind of flashy tackling that allows a striker to get behind them—there's likely to be no defender between that striker and the goal. Sweepers are the last players back. If the opposing goalie has a strong punt, or if the opposing team likes to play a long ball, be sure to mark your opponent a safe distance behind him. You cannot afford a fast one-on-one chase for the ball with a speedy striker when the ball is heading toward your own goal.

TIPS FROM THE STARS: PLAYING DEFENSE

The thing for defenders to avoid? *Don't dive in*—don't go making a gallant rush for the ball. That's just what the forward wants you to do. You dive in, and he's gone. Hold with him . . . dog him . . . go sideways . . . push the man to the outside (if he goes wide he's got to cross, and you can still get your body in front). Always force the play to the outside. When it's time for you to bring the ball up, *you* should go outside as well.

Never get caught "ball watching." Ball watching is the worst mistake that any soccer player can make. You should never let your man out of your sight for a moment. You have to know where the ball is, but *don't let yourself get sucked into watching the play when you should always be watching your man!* Never take your eye off your man, not for an instant. If you are caught in a two-on-one give-and-go situation, watch your *man,* not the ball. Stay with your man. If you don't, no one else will.

Get away from diving in—avoid the sliding tackle whenever you can. It should be used only as a desperation play, to save your team from a breakaway or a shot. Don't try to win a ball on a sliding tackle. Jockey your man; hold him; let your team recover so that every man is marked. Whenever possible, *stay on your feet!*

Defenders should avoid making wild clearances. Don't go booming it out. *Push it out,* push it out to your teammates. Attack from the back is the style of modern soccer. Concentrate on the needs of the team, not your own ball handling. A long ball is good when it's the only thing you can do (say, when an opponent is right there on you) or to break up the pressure of a constant attack. Otherwise, forget the long ball.

Bobby Smith

The wing fullbacks should move up when the opportunity presents itself. Often the best time is when the ball is on the opposite side of the field. Then the players tend to push up and bunch up on the side where the ball is, and you've got free space to work with. When the wing pulls over to the middle, you can often generate a breakaway by charging into that open space. The hardest thing about going up-field as a fullback is learning how to read the play. Always be aware both of what you can do by pushing up and of the *risks* you take by leaving the backfield. Each time you push forward, try to analyze what happens and to learn from it.

Steve Ralbovsky

Fullbacks are no longer the "bigfoot" toughs of the soccer field. Fullbacks are now playmakers, even strikers on occasion. But every fullback should remember that his first priority is to defend his goal.

THE MIDFIELDERS

The midfielders, or linkmen, are responsible for the middle of the field. But when the situation demands it, they can become forwards and they can become fullbacks. Linkmen must be versatile (dribblers, passers, shooters, defenders), and they probably need a greater level of endurance than is required in any other soccer position. Depending upon the strategy and the alignment that the team uses, the midfielders are called halfbacks, upcenter fullbacks, dropped insides, or liberos. For the purposes of this discussion, we'll call all the midfielders "halfs."

For midfielders are just that. Halfway between offense and defense, controlling the halfway area of the field, playing about equal amounts of time on offense and defense. Good halfs are like a communications network, relaying the ball from the defense up to the forwards, and switching it around as much as necessary in the process.

If you intend to play a midfield position, a half, be prepared to run all day. There is probably not a single instant in an entire soccer game in which a half should not be running. Forwards tend to cover about half of the field, and fullbacks (unless they have come up for offensive play, which is not the rule) tend to cover the other half. But a half must cover two-thirds of the field in the ordinary course of play, and he may be called upon to run the *entire* length of the field many times during a game. Halfs start the offensive play at midfield. When they have moved the ball up to the forwards, they should always follow up the play, remaining just behind their strikers to take a backward pass or to intercept an attempted defensive clearance.

Then, when the opposition is on offense, the halfs must dog the opposing forwards at midfield, and move back with the play all the way into the territory of their own fullbacks.

The half's position is an active one, requiring speed, stamina, intelligence, awareness, anticipation, aggressiveness at some times, and caution at other times. It is also the most expressive and improvisational position on the field. The half is always making choices—his actions are not dictated by the position of the ball on the field nearly as much as by that of the other players. The half's options are almost infinite. Upon taking control of the ball, a half might send it down to his wing or cross it over to the other wing; or he might tap the ball over to another half; or he could backheel it to his fullback and move forward for a return pass; or, if the way is clear, he might dribble the ball into the opposition's territory, drawing one or more defenders to him and setting up a shot on goal.

With so many choices in disposing of the ball—back, forward, side, keep, pass—the half must be keenly tuned in to the locations of his teammates and of the opposition players. Passes should always go to an open teammate, and the half should follow up his pass by moving to an open space to support the teammate who receives the ball. A pass to an inside, follow-up, reception of a pass back, and then a pass out to the unmarked wing are often the pivotal precedents to a scoring play.

Watch the defenders. When they have pulled back into the goal area, you should feel free to move closer to the goal. If they are spread out, you need to hang back a bit to intercept attempted defensive clearances. Halfs function to keep the ball in the opposition half of the field. Don't be afraid to use your fullbacks for that purpose, going backward with a pass to open up space, then moving into position for a return pass. Look for free wings. You can be extremely useful if you send the ball down to an open wing or if you cross the ball when the play is too congested on one side of the field.

Be aware of your fullbacks even if you're not "using" them. When a fullback makes a charge up into the defense, it's your responsibility to move back and cover for him. If the opposition is bringing the ball up in midfield, your own options depend on the location of the fullback. If your defender is properly positioned, you can afford to move in aggressively, to commit yourself, and to try to take the ball from the forwards. If your defender is out of position, you will have to play a more cautious game, containing and slowing down the forwards until your defender is able to back you up for a move that might take you out of the play altogether. If the opposition should get the ball past you, don't stand around assuming that you are no longer part of the play. Run back. Mark a player. Bring yourself back into the action as fast as you possibly can. Make yourself important. Take the initiative. That's the key to good link play—to never let up, to always find a way to become involved in the action, to be aware of defenders on your side and forwards on theirs, to switch from defense to offense and back again within seconds, and to run, run, run, run, run. The opposition should see you as a plague, and your own team should see you as a pony express.

TIPS FROM THE STARS: PLAYING MIDFIELD

At forward you can sometimes afford to lose the ball by taking a chance, but never at midfield. Midfielders are playmakers—they get things going. They shouldn't really take an opponent on too much, but contain him. Having played fullback, midfield, and wing, I know that most goals come on a ball that has been lost at midfield—this gives the other team a chance for a fast break.

The worst thing that can happen to a midfielder, aside from losing the ball, is to get caught out of position. Midfielders should play *simple and safe*—a plain game aimed at *keeping possession of the ball above all.* Don't dive in—be a ball distributor, a playmaker, and a defenseman. The *first* task of a midfielder is defense (but of course the midfielder must play offense too, so you must learn to switch at a moment's notice). Midfielders should be just as cautious in defense as fullbacks—contain your opponent, avoid going off your feet. Even though there's a man behind you, you can't afford to take yourself out of the play, because this overloads the fullbacks. Slow the other team down; force mistakes. And again, be plain and simple.

Steve Ralbovsky

The game relies so much on improvisation. As a midfielder your emphasis should be on containment—you certainly don't want to leave the backfield shorthanded. Who your opponent is determines whether you play a pressure-game or a containment game. Listen for commands coming from the defenders behind you. If everybody is marked you can pressure your man, but not if you are outnumbered or not in defensive control. Always realize what's going on in terms of who is marking whom. Drive the play to the outside as much as you can. Most teams are strongest up the middle. Always keep your body between the man and the goal. When you keep the opposing player to the outside he is limited in space.

If the ball is on your side of the field and you have the space in front of you, go all the way up. If you have the ball carry it down into space and create the play. Midfielders always come up from behind for support. Go up and support the man with the ball. When your team is on offense, be offensive-minded.

In the NASL the pressure is now on the midfielder to interchange roles, different roles, not just stay in the middle of the field. Midfielders must now be stronger defensive players. The stereotype of the "middleman" is now over. Midfielders go to all other positions, more so than anybody else. Midfielders are generally the playmakers and directors of the play in the NASL, more and more. The midfielder is in play more than anyone else and must be a good team leader.

Al Trost

THE FORWARDS (THE WINGS, THE INSIDES, THE CENTER FORWARD)

The job of the forwards is to move the ball to the opposing goal area and to score. That may seem obvious, but it should never be forgotten. Forwards must have all the skills that are required to play good soccer, but the most skillful forward is useless unless he can move the ball into position for a shot *and take the shot*. In other words, the key to an effective set of forwards is *aggressiveness*. Defenders and midfielders can play a relatively restrained, contained game and still serve a team well.

Forwards cannot. Forwards must overwhelm the defense physically and psychologically, or they will never score. Speed is of the essence, speed and teamwork, confidence, and assertiveness. The forward must act without hesitation, or he will not have the opportunity to act at all.

The Wings

The wing, or "outside," must be a speedster above all. He is probably the fastest runner on the team, and his speed is used to get the ball behind the opposing defense. In traditional play, the wing was a player who waited at midfield for the ball and, upon receiving it, drove pell-mell down the line toward the goal, finishing off his run with a cross in front of the goal to his waiting forwards, who promptly headed it into the nets. This is still a viable role for the wing, though the wing is now a much freer, more expressive player.

The touchline run with the ball is spectacular and effective. The wing must be both fast and a good ball handler, for in this play controlled speed is everything. The touchline serves as a limit—the wing must keep the ball in bounds—but it also provides a singular advantage. The wing knows that no one can challenge him from the outside. This means that long, sustained runs are possible if the wing can gain a step on his defender at the outset. The defender will remain with him, close enough to keep other defenders from coming to help, but the defender will not be able to get the ball. The wing cannot be "blind-sided" because there *is* no blind side. Wings should always try to fake a play to the inside, for if the defender is thrown off, a run down the touchline is one of the most potent means of penetration in soccer.

The touchline run also provides a useful means of changing pace while retaining control in the event that the winger's forward progress is stopped. Wings should learn how to use the out-of-bounds safety valve that is right next to them. A quick kick of the ball against your opponent's legs will put the ball out-of-bounds, with a throw-in for your team. You have retained possession of the ball, and as a winger, you can reposition yourself downfield, with another player taking the throw-in.

After moving the ball deep into the opposition territory, you must put the icing on the cake with an effective cross. This is one cake that is worthless without the icing. Crosses are of two types: general and specific. The specific cross, which is basically a pass to a free teammate, is always the best play. But sometimes you will have only a general idea of where the ball should go. You may be unsure of exactly where your teammates are heading, or the defense may have clogged up the goal area to such an extent that you are unable to execute a cross with precision. The general cross is not a pointless kick, however, as any major coach will tell you, because it tends to *create* scoring situations that did not exist at the moment of the pass. More "garbage" goals are scored by crosses that are directed, not to a player, but to a place where the defense is vulnerable, than by any other kind of play. The role of such "garbage" goals should not be underestimated. For if your team does score often, and win games, it has probably been manufacturing garbage goals as often as possible.

In the specific cross, you, as a winger, pick out a teammate and pass the ball directly to him. This is generally a sideways pass, although you may (and you should always be aware of this possibility) choose to send the ball back to your following half if he is clear and has good position. Your pass should be careful—you are in the midst of the opposing defense, and the defenders are *looking* for the pass, trying to anticipate it, so your pass must be accurate and controllable. Your receiving teammate may be in a scoring position or simply in a good, dangerous spot. Don't rush to pass to the teammate in the scoring position if you've got another teammate in a strategic spot who will find it easier to control the ball and to move it to yet another forward. Sometimes it's best to work the ball a bit and to "close in" for the score, rather than hurry the shot precipitously. On your crosses, always look for the specific pass, to a specific teammate, as your first alternative. Too many wings feel that they have discharged their responsibilities by blasting the ball across the goal from the corner in which they have just barely avoided trapping themselves. Not so. After penetration, the pass should be *to a teammate* whenever possible. Watch the pros play, on television or in person. You'll see that the wing almost invariably plays the ball to a specific man. Ignore the exhortations of inexpe-

When the ball is crossed to you, be prepared to send it even farther across the field or to switch directions entirely, and be ready to do this on the volley, without a trap. Here the receiver's mind is half on his reception and half on the new direction in which he will send the ball—and that is as it must be.

Learn to turn the ball at right angles when it comes in on the cross. Often you'll have to twist your body in midair to do this.

rienced players and coaches who shout, "Cross the ball! Cross the ball!" They should be urging you to *pass* the ball, not cross it.

But as we all know, the direct or specific pass is not always possible. And the advantage of having the ball deep in opposition territory should never be lost. When there is no pass, or when you are moving so fast that a specific pass would mean a damaging slowdown of the play, a general cross, properly executed, is by all means better than nothing at all. When you place the ball in front of the goal you create a volatile situation in which your teammates might score. Never pass up such an opportunity. Goals are scored when forwards have a chance to shoot on goal, not when a wing, dogged by an angry fullback, winds up diddling with the ball in the corner of the field.

When the general cross is in the air, as most will be, it should always be aimed to fall on a line with the far goalpost. If your cross lands in the vicinity of the near goalpost, your teammate

will usually have to turn the ball, rather than merely meet it or intercept it, in order to get off a shot. This makes the shooting angle much more difficult, and unnecessarily so. When the ball goes toward the far post, a forward can head it by moving directly into the ball, changing its direction *with power*, or kick it by moving straight into the ball. Power and accuracy of shot are much better served by a cross that goes across the goal. In addition, this kind of cross throws off the defense. When you have the ball outside, the defense is oriented toward your side of the field. This includes the goalie, who, if he is playing properly, will probably be on your side of the goal. A cross across the goal forces the defense, the goalie included, to scramble to the other side of the goal to block the shot. Once the defense is scrambling, your team is really on the offense. The opposition is off balance, confused, hesitant, out of position— all of the things you want them to be. Your cross may be a hard ground ball, a chip.

a lofted ball, or a sharp, low line drive. It all depends upon the situation, upon the location of your teammates and of the defenders. The one thing you want to *avoid* is using a *habitual* kind of cross (for example, always lofting the ball for the far post). By doing this, you fail to take into account the specifics of the given situation, and you give the defense a predictive edge, since the defense will always know what you are going to do. This advice goes for every aspect of your game, no matter what position you play. *Avoid habitual patterns.*

Wings today do much more than wait at midfield for a ball that they can carry down the touchline. Now wings learn to *go* for the ball, not merely wait for it, by harassing defenders, making tackles, and anticipating and intercepting passes. When the ball is on the opposite side of the field, it is no longer necessary for the wing to remain on the touchline. Move in toward the goal; make yourself an extra inside. You will not help the team on offense if you remain outside when the ball is being worked in toward the goal. Many goals are now scored from the post by a wing who has taken his pass from the *other* wing.

Though wings now move inside with the play, and work more aggressively to gain the ball rather than waiting passively to receive it, they should still patrol the offensive part of the field. Resist the temptation to come back too far on defense, even if your team is being consistently pressured. You are needed out at the halfway mark, for when your teammates take possession of the ball they must have some forward players to pass up to. Unless you await the pass, they will be trapped, perhaps losing the ball to the pressing opposition when a passing outlet is unavailable. So you must function as an escape valve when your team is on defense, a ground gainer when you have the ball, a crosser when you are near the goal, and a scoring inside when the ball is on the opposite side of the field and coming across. Your main job is to move the ball downfield and *behind* the opposing defense, but a good wing will also take pride in performing the other tasks well. If he does, he will be a much greater asset to the team than the fast wing who only wants to make his sideline runs with the ball.

The Inside Forwards (the Insides and the Center Forward)

The inside forwards, also called the strikers, are the main goal scorers of the team. They must be quick, agile ball handlers, good passers, and able to take shots from a variety of positions without hesitation. The difference between a good striker and a bad one is often told in the fraction of an instant in which the bad striker hesitates before shooting.

Forwards must lack none of the important offensive skills. A forward must be a good dribbler and fake artist—often a quick move that throws a defender off for a split second makes the difference between a goal and a lost chance. Forwards must be accurate and fearless headers too, since heading on a cross is a key source of goals. Strikers should also make themselves proficient in the skills of volleying, first-time kicking, and overhead (or bicycle) kicking.

The insides are total players. They must be keenly aware of the pattern of action in the center of the field, always taking the best possible position, working with the halfbacks, and moving back to help on defense. The play of an inside can be conceptualized as being that of a halfback, only more forward. The insides are the real playmakers of the team. They constantly create spaces and move into new spaces. Insides must be able to kick well with both feet and to place a pass with pinpoint accuracy. If an attack can never quite jell for a team, the insides are probably to blame.

The insides must master all of the skills and tactics involved in "moving the ball," from light and accurate dribbling to backheeling, to give-and-go, to setting up a pick. And the insides are the players who must make *sure* that the ball *stays* on the offense when it is being played offensively. They must scrap, and they must commit themselves fully to retaking the ball from a defender who gains possession. They must dog the play as the defense tries to move the ball back upfield. They should always rush the goalie on the chance that he will miss the ball, and they should guard the goalie on goal kicks when the keeper and a fullback may be trying to work out a strategic play. Like halfbacks, insides must be able to run all day.

The inside is a scrapper. Though the inside must be a good and controlled ball handler, above all he must be *aggressive*. If there is a loose ball in midfield or near the goal area, it should be the inside who picks it up. Many goals are scored only because of the sheer aggressiveness of the insides. The insides should be able to set up plays, to shoot immediately when the opportunity presents itself, and above all, through their aggressiveness, to *create* shooting opportunities for themselves and their teammates.

Here the shot is aimed for the upper corner of the goal. The nonkicking knee points in the intended direction of the ball. The follow-through is complete, with the toe pointed slightly upward, again in the intended direction of the shot. A slight lean-back helps to propel the ball upward (above). When you can't reach the ball standing up, slide into it. This is especially true for a cross in which accuracy is not a prime consideration. In front of the goal, a weak foot on the ball is usually better than no foot at all (below).

TIPS FROM THE STARS: PLAYING FORWARD

If I were teaching a youngster how to play forward, the first thing I would say is, "Learn to play defense." You're on defense when your team loses the ball, no matter where you play. Learn to play both ways at a young age. When the other team gains possession, the first thing the forward should do is get back on the goal side of the two middle fullbacks—get in between them, and force them to go to one side of the field or the other, but keep them from going up the middle. *Delay* the counterattack. A forward should not dive in and commit himself on defense even though there is a man behind him. The forward should contain the man, dog him, make the opposing side play the ball and, hopefully, make a mistake. Part of the game is taking a few chances, and a forward is a little freer to do that, but really you should just go for containment. Mark the attacking fullback, the one who brings the ball upfield. If he goes all the way into the goalie box, as a Beckenbauer might, you have to go all the way back with him. Wherever the forward fullback goes, the forward follows. You become the valuable extra man on defense, but don't go far back unless you are following the fullback who has come up.

The instant your team takes possession, you, the forward, must get open. You look for space, and you go wherever it is. Move into any space where you're going to be open. If the pass comes to you at midfield, lay it off to someone else, perhaps the man who passed it to you, and make a run into the corner—*don't dribble* until you are in the attacking third of the field. In midfield, one-touch the ball and keep it moving. Get the defense leaning—go beyond faking and see where the defense *expects* you to go, give a fake that way, then switch. Use a decoy man, use a give-and-go. You must *create* a good angle for an open shot on goal. Never move the ball in a straight line—always try to move it at angles.

Greg Villa

The Center Forward

The center forward is the central player on offense and, like the wings, he has primarily offensive responsibilities, with a minimal defensive involvement. He runs the offense—he's the leader. He should be a good ball handler, a scrapper, fast, and intelligent. All of his energies should be devoted to the scoring of goals and the creation of scoring opportunities. He must play with confidence and strength and enjoy outwitting the opponents' defense. His trapping must be excellent on any type of pass, for he probably receives more crucial passes than does any other player. Too, the center forward will be shooting more than any other player. He must develop the ability to place a strong first-time kick without any hesitation. He must be able to kick over his head, behind his back, upside down, and inside out. Since the center forward will often be shooting with the goalie directly in front of him, he must learn to shoot off the side of his foot so that the ball will enter the goal at an angle even when the center forward is at the middle of the goal.

To be most effective, a center forward should rarely enter the defensive half of the field. He must be the "leading edge" for a fast break when his team gains offensive possession of the ball. When the goalie makes a long kick over the heads of the opposing fullbacks, the center forward should be there to take the ball. In most alignments, and for most strategies, the center forward should hang at about midfield. This doesn't mean that he shouldn't play defensively and try to steal the ball when the opposing team is bringing the ball up from its own defensive territory. He should indeed go after the ball. In fact, the center forward should be most aggressive about trying to pick up balls from the opposition. He is mainly an offensive player. If he commits himself and misses, this will not disrupt the defense. If he should succeed he may well open up a fast break and a score for his team.

TIPS FROM THE STARS: PLAYING FORWARD

As I see it, scoring a goal is the main object of the game, the only object of the game. It's not easy, you have to be fortunate. There's a bit of luck involved, but you have to make your luck. Center forward is the most difficult role on the field. You're always marked, your back is to the goal, your back is to the defenders, you have the disadvantage of only being able to go for that small, small target—the goal.

Try to kick first time. Try to kick as soon as you get it. Learn how to kick on the fly. I always use as much force as possible and let the ball fly. You can't score if you don't shoot. Keep the ball low, because it's so much more difficult for the keeper to bend down. Never forget your object is to score goals. Be on the lookout for the free ball and go to it, get it! Body fakes are your main tools. Pull the defenders off to the side if you can, even before the ball comes. You only need a split second to shoot, but you must get that split second. Vary your play. Don't be predictable. Learn to be quick off the mark so you can get the ball before the defender does.

Scoring, playing forward, is so much instinct. You've got to work at actually developing your instinct. You're a kind of animal, a scoring animal. Only one thing must be in your mind—scoring goals. You must figure out ways to get away from your opponent—don't be lazy, above all— then you can use your skills. Get free, shoot fast, that's the essence of it.

Giorgio Chinaglia

You always try to go to the goal the quickest way. You try to create danger, try to take the ball into the penalty box. Get in there as quickly as you can, because anything can happen. If you are looking dangerous, defensive players see the danger and try to stop it. And sometimes, trying to stop it, they can knock you over, and you can get a penalty kick. Get into the goal area as soon as you can, and hold the ball. Even if he doesn't catch you and you go by him, maybe you have one or two teammates behind you who can play the ball into the net.

I try to maneuver defenders out of the box, because the box is very congested. If you go by one man, then another man has to come out to cut off the danger. If he comes out, someone on your team must be there to receive the pass.

When you are marked, what you learn to do is occupy your man. If someone is marking you, take him to another opponent, and then you are occupying two people. Take the man who is marking you right up to the sweeper, because the sweeper isn't marking anyone. The sweeper just wants to be by himself, and he doesn't want anybody near him.

Jimmy Johnstone

The Positions in General

The role of any player depends upon the alignment, the strategy, and the style of play of his team. There is no such thing as a "rule" about the right way to play any single position. It all depends on the kind of game your team is playing. You must play in the way that best serves your team, not in the way that you think is "right" for the position. For there are many "right" ways. What's right, in essence, is what works.

Your position is only a place on the field, not a statement about your abilities at one skill or another. Don't feel that you shouldn't or can't dribble simply because you are a fullback, for example. But *do* be aware of the consequences, ramifications, dangers, and advantages of being a dribbling fullback as opposed to, say, a dribbling wing. To everything there is a season, and to every place on the field there is an appropriate way of playing according to the lay of the action.

The main thing, as you will see in "Working the Ball" (Chapter 5) and "Alignments and Tactics" (Chapter 8), is that the members of a team must relate to one another. The team works as a unit, and the separate areas of the field work as subunits. The wing, for example, must always work with the halfback behind him, the inside alongside him, and the fullback behind him. This foursome should be in constant communication, verbally and through the language of movement. The relationship of players in the smaller units of the field is what transforms a soccer club from a bunch of individual players into a team that can move and control the ball. The units work together within themselves, and the units connect up and work with each other. In this way the ball is moved in one part of the field, then switched and moved in another part of the field. Players pass, not in panic, but by instinct because each player knows where the other players are and what the other players will do. The smoothly functioning machine that is a soccer team, whether it be on the professional level or on the grammar school level, can only exist when the players are profoundly involved in this relatedness and working together. There is always room for the star, of course, but the star can work only from the base of a tightly knit and related team. Even Pele could not make the Cosmos win until they learned (and were rearranged) to work together.

5
Working the Ball

THE PROCESS OF PASSING

The organic flow that is necessary to good soccer comes, as any experienced player knows, from a smoothly rhythmic pattern of accurate and intelligent passing. But how do you generate the kind of team control and movement that the pros make look so easy? There are indeed separable ingredients in this kind of integrated play: players must develop the necessary passing and receiving skills, learn to relate to the players near them and to the rest of the players on the team, learn to move into open spaces in order to create an outlet for a pass to themselves or to free up another player, learn to support the player with the ball, and learn to pass quickly and without hesitation. In addition, there are special kinds of passes and plays that can be learned easily on the practice field for use in game situations. And there is a passing style appropriate to defensive situations as well as one that is right when you are on offense.

We have already discussed kicking and receiving skills in Chapter 3. Now let's look at some of the kinds of passes and at the player configurations that make those passes work best. We

will deal both with passing methods and with methods of movement that free up a team's passing potential.

Basic Passing

Passes must be both controlled and controllable. A pass that hits your player on the button is worthless if it is kicked too hard for him to handle effectively. By the same token, a slow pass that is easy to handle is also easy to intercept and may disrupt the needed quick rhythm of play. So your passes must reach for a happy medium—fast enough to keep the ball moving, yet not too difficult to handle. The way to achieve that happy medium is to *keep the ball on the ground*. Few balls that are rolling on the grass will be too hot to handle, no matter how fast they are traveling—ground balls are by far the easiest to trap. You can pass the ball hard and sharp—fast enough to avoid interception— if you keep it on the ground. Because ground balls remain under control, your receiver will be able to trap the ball if necessary, and he will also have the option of simply running behind it or flicking it. It is particularly important to keep your passes on the ground during wet weather, when control of the ball becomes an even more difficult art.

To keep the ball on the ground, be sure to have your weight forward as you kick it. Leaning back tends to make a ball loft upward. Too, you should contact the ball at its midpoint or higher—scooping under the ball will also loft it. All but the most skillful and experienced players will find that *the way to keep passes both accurate and on the ground is to kick with the side of the foot.*

The side-of-the-foot kick is really the passing kick. Until you are a truly expert passer you should try to make *all* of your passes with the side of your foot. Long passes are, of course, going to require a standard instep kick, but if you and your team are playing properly, long passes are by far the exception, not the rule. The rule is passes of short and intermediate length, all of which are most accurately executed with a side-of-the-foot kick.

The precise kind of pass you use is not nearly as important as the fact that *the pass should not present too great a control problem to the player who receives it.* This is only logical. What good is a pass if your teammate will inevitably lose it? The whole idea of a *pass* is that it should be a *transfer of possession* of the ball from you to your teammate.

True, there are all kinds of passes—short taps, backheels, chips, lofting kicks down to a wing, and so on. But until you and your team are working as a smoothly functioning machine, try to limit your passes to side-of-the-foot ground balls that are accurate and easy to handle. No bounces, no line drives, no bigfoot boots. Just short, crisp passes that skim the surface of the grass like a golf putt.

Effective passing rests on your ability to *do something* with the ball when you get it, to know where your teammates are, and to move into an open, available space when you have not got the ball so that a pass may come to you. If each player moves the ball off to a free teammate quickly, if each player has the "split vision" to control the ball and still know where the offense and the defense are playing, and if

Here the close pass will go to the outside into an unchallenged space and away from the defender. Even Pele would have trouble interfering with two players who are maintaining such tight control.

each player puts himself into position to receive a pass whenever possible, your team will move the ball and your team will win soccer matches.

When your teammate has the ball, you *must* create a passing outlet for him. You must watch the defenders and move to an area in which your teammate can pass to you with a clear angle. You cannot simply watch him dribbling or looking for a pass. *The key to the whole game of soccer is moving to an open space so that you can receive a pass.* If you have the ball, and your teammates simply jog around waiting to see what you're going to do with it, you'll find yourself trapped more times than not. Everyone must move to help out the player with the ball, everyone must give him *support*.

Support means shaking off your defender so that you can take a pass. Support means coming up behind your teammate with the ball and letting him know that you are there for a backward pass. Support means positioning yourself laterally to take a pass when the defender is right in front of your ball carrier. You must talk to the teammate with the ball, let him know where you are and what you are doing. If you want to break to a space for the ball, call out to him. Tell him to lead you with a pass. If you have the ball, you must always be *looking for the pass*. This is the crucial aspect of the game that most novice players overlook. *The instant you get the ball you should be looking for your pass.*

Remember, no defender can possibly move as fast as you can pass the ball. For that reason, team play, team movement, must always rely on a smooth flow of passing.

The Wall Pass

This pass is extremely useful in soccer. It takes its name from the practice of English boys who traditionally learned soccer in the alleyways of industrial cities. A savvy youngster soon learned that one of the best ways to get past a boy defending against him was to pass the ball at an angle against the alley wall, run around the defender, and retrieve the ball behind the defender.

The wall pass is essentially the same as the give-and-go of basketball. Instead of passing to

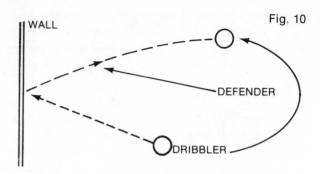

Fig. 10

a wall, you will be passing to one of your teammates. The moment you pass, you run behind the defender who is marking you to take a return pass from your teammate. Your defender will be momentarily confused because you no longer have the ball, and he will not be guarding you as tightly as he was. This gives you the instant you need to get behind him after you have passed off to your teammate. The wall pass makes a triangle with two players, and it can also be executed in a sequence involving several players, like this:

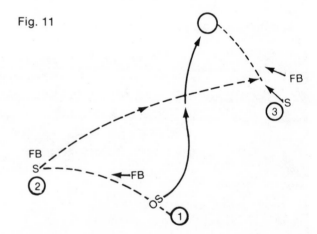

Fig. 11

Learn to execute wall passes in series, with players forming and reforming the triangles, and you will watch your team cut through opposing defenses like a hot knife through butter.

The Pick

Picks are another type of pass that is similar to the style of play in basketball. Here, instead of passing the ball off to your teammate and running behind your defender, you use the mere physical presence of your teammate to create an

A "footoff," leaving the ball off for Pele, who is coming up behind, and taking out the defender—all in one simple, small, quick move (above). The wall pass leads the receiver in tune with his running speed. The passer then turns forward to become the new receiver, and the receiver becomes the passer (below).

This pass to the "wall" is to be followed up with a run and a return pass. The first pass stays to the clear side of the receiver.

opening through which you may move the ball. Picks are of two types—the handoff, which in soccer might better be called the "footoff," and the reversal.

In the "footoff," your teammate has the ball with his back to the defender. You come running by very close to him and take a quick little pass right past both him and his defender. He has blocked out the defender by merely being there, and any opponent who is marking you will not have enough room to squeeze in and interfere with the play (without committing a foul). Footoffs can occur in many situations, but generally they look like this:

Fig. 12

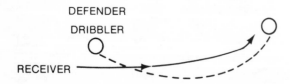

The reversal is like the reverse in football or the key-pick in basketball. The ball carrier moves in one direction—usually it is a lateral move—and is blocked by defenders from pushing farther. The pass receiver comes up behind his teammate, running in the opposite direction. When the pass receiver is moving in this way, no defender can tightly mark him. Where the ball and the defenders had previously been moving in the direction of the ball carrier, suddenly the motion of the play is reversed. The element of surprise works in your favor, and the play almost invariably yields a free ball carrier with sufficient space for effective maneuvering. When your teammate has the ball and is coming toward you, the correct play is often to move away from him and into an open space. But you will frequently be able to throw the defense off guard by moving *to* your teammate and taking the ball behind him, as he shields you from the defender:

Fig. 13

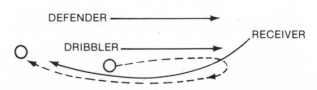

Teams must learn to press forward in a given direction; they must also learn to execute a strategic surprise reversal when an area is clotted with defenders.

The Through or Penetrating Pass

The ability to complete perfect through passes is the most important and the most effective characteristic of a winning soccer team. The through pass means breakaways and goals.

The through pass is a pass in which you slice through the opposing defense, and the key to successful through passing is timing. The through pass does not go directly *to* the intended receiver. It *leads* him—leads him into open spaces and freedom. The ball goes *through* the opposing players to a point that your teammate has not yet reached. But your teammate runs to that point just as you are passing, and he picks up the ball that had been rolling toward a seeming no one. He heads the ball off at the pass, so to speak.

Basically, the through pass looks like this:

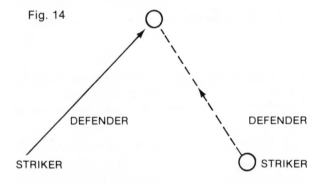

Fig. 14

The through pass is the most potent way of putting the ball behind your opponents' defenses. Most soccer teams do not fear a team that only passes the ball back and forth in front of the defenders—such play can be contained. But the through pass makes the opposition vulnerable. If your team learns to connect with through passes at will, the opposition will be nervous, cautious, literally on the defensive. And that *psychological* edge can make the difference between winning and losing.

Obviously, in effecting the through pass, *timing* is of the essence. The passer must time his pass so as to avoid defenders and yet must push the ball into an open space just when his receiver is about to break free. If the pass comes

too early, the receiver may be unable to reach it and the ball will be picked up by the defense. If the pass comes too late, the receiver may well find himself offside. The receiver must time his move to the passer too. If the receiver moves too early, the passer may not have a proper angle or the receiver may telegraph the play to the defenders. The receiver must watch his passer carefully, tune in to him, so that the penetrating pass meets him at the precise moment when he is clear behind the defense.

For the through pass to be timed properly, both the passer and the receiver must be in communication. Each can call to the other, either verbally ("Over here") or through some form of code so that the defense will not be tipped off to the play. If the passer and the receiver can make eye contact, communication without calling out is possible, and this usually works even better than calling out, since the defense is not alerted. Hand signals can also be used. The very best system for executing through passes, though, is to work on them thoroughly in practice until they become a habitual way of playing. Then, *whenever* a penetrating pass is possible, the passer will be attempting to make the pass and the receiver will be making himself open to receive it. Without any calling or deciding, the through pass will be made because it is the right play for the situation.

Running off the Ball

One key to the success of any team is what the players do when they *don't* have the ball. Even the greatest ball handler will be stymied if his teammates do not give him support by moving to open spaces *and* by pulling off the defense through decoy maneuvers.

We have already spoken about the need to "make yourself open" on the field, always moving so that the ball carrier will have a clear angle to pass to you. And the point cannot be stressed enough. Great soccer teams are made not so much by outstanding ball handling as by what is done by the players who are not on the ball, perhaps not even near it. If your teammate is forced to dribble because he does not have a clear pass, your team will lose the ball. And if

Even before his teammate receives the ball, the outside player is running off the ball to get into position for a pass. Note the "entrapment" shape of the receiver.

you and your teammates cannot get clear to move the ball in nice, controlled patterns, your team will never be able to get behind the defense and work in for the score. Players do not usually realize this until they have reached a fairly high level of expertise, but there is no reason why the most inexperienced team member cannot learn and follow this most basic precept—*you are always "playing" on the soccer field, even if the ball is nowhere near you.*

A very effective role for players who are not in possession of the ball—one that's not in as common use as it should be—is that of decoy. The decoy player runs to draw defenders off the play, or off the space where the play is supposed to go. The truly valuable player on a soccer team is the one who will make unselfish runs to help his teammate, even if he is not running in order to be able to receive the ball. For example, the player with the ball may be facing a single defender whom he may well be able to beat in a one-on-one situation. But the teammate of the player with the ball is behind this

defender, marked by another defender. If the player with the ball gets past defender 1, defender 2, now guarding his teammate, will be there waiting for him. So the teammate makes a run, hoping to draw defender 2 with him. If he does, the player with the ball will have free space in which to work with the ball. If defender 2 does not follow the teammate, then the ball carrier has a free pass.

Even if you are closely guarded, then, you should *always be running to change the configuration of the spaces on the field.* By drawing a defender with you, you may be able to create a two-on-one situation for the player with the ball and another teammate. This is the kind of move that helps score goals, even if you never touch the ball.

Movement off the ball can be very creative. Let's say that there is a throw-in and that you see that your wing is free for the throw. Before the defenders have a chance to notice this and cover him, you distract them by running into a space and calling loud and long for the ball. The focus of attention shifts to you for an instant, the wing remains free, the throw goes to him, and he makes a break down the touchline. Similarly, on a free kick your team might have a player run in front of the defensive wall calling for the ball, thus distracting the defense and taking one or two players with him. In this way he creates a space for another player who slips in quietly behind him, to the space he has just left.

Often a good decoy play merely involves taking a run that switches you from your customary position. A wing moving to the inside will often confuse the fullback marking him. If the fullback follows, the wing space is left open for the offensive fullback who can come charging through. If the fullback remains in his area, you have an extra player inside to help work the ball. This kind of running to break free of the defense sets up situations in which the defense is off guard, off balance, confused, and vulnerable to your team play.

If you want to really help your team and really stand out as a good soccer player, always ask yourself, "Where can I go now? How can I help the ball carrier, how can I pull the defense out of equilibrium, how can I get free for a pass?" Your play without the ball is just as important as your play with the ball.

TIPS FROM THE STARS: RUNNING AWAY FROM THE PLAY

I like to make runs. I like to sneak up on opponents. Sneak up from behind. I like to get in on the blind side even if I have to run fifty or sixty yards. Most of my goals come because I have great endurance and I can make these long runs even at the end of a game. Get in on the blind side, away from the play. The key to this kind of play is being fit. Go where the play isn't, moving into and taking space even though it's far away from you. Try to be deceptive. Learn to sprint fifty yards fast. And sprint with the ball, too, attack the defenders with the ball and look for a quick give and go.

Al Trost

THE GENERAL WAY OF MOVEMENT

As you watch a world class team move the ball downfield or ease it out of a defensive situation, you notice that the ball develops a rhythm of movement. The play tends to go in a zigzag fashion, with a pass to the left, then to the right, then perhaps two more passes to the left, one back, one to the right again. The play flows constantly to where the receivers are and the defenders are not. When your team has the ball, there are fundamental patterns that you can form to ensure that as many players as possible will be available to receive the ball. Through these patterns the players establish a mode of mutual support by their very presence on the field.

Subunits

The team must break itself down into subunits, and each subunit must move together as a single force. If you will recall, we spoke in the introduction of the team as eleven players who are, in effect, repeated images of each other. When the ball is moved down the touchline, for example, you have a subunit composed of the wing, the wing half, the wing fullback, and perhaps the center half and inside. These players must all work together and must take the advantage as it presents itself. If the fullback has a chance to charge through, the wing will hang back a bit to provide support behind. Or perhaps the half will drop back and take up a more defensive role. Whatever the case, these players should keep their interchangeability in mind, and not restrict themselves to the mechanical boundaries implied by the position names of "wing" or "half." Depending upon where the play goes, any player can and should, at least for the duration of a specific sequence, take up *any* position. It is simply not enough to say, "I play position X, and I have fulfilled my responsibilities, and that's all I have to do." You should always be looking for something *more* that you can do, and you should always maintain the flexibility to temporarily assume any position on the field when the situation demands it.

The subunits should always travel together.

The fastest wing is helpless without the support of his inside and his half, and often his fullback. In general, all of the players in a unit (a unit usually consists of the three or four players closest to the ball) should travel in a triangular or square shape. Triangulation and squaring are what really help players get free consistently for the methodical interpassing forward movement that makes up most of a properly played game.

Triangles and Squares

As you come to support the ball carrier, you should place yourself in alignment with the other players so as to form a square or a triangle. Squares and triangles will always be effective in freeing up a receiver, except if your team is being perfectly marked in a tight player-to-player manner. In that case, picks and reversals will set you free.

Let's say that your player with the ball is moving upfield with a teammate beside him. You want to give the player with the ball as many potential passing angles as possible. He surely doesn't need yet another teammate alongside him. In order to provide the greatest number of passing angles for him, you should position yourself behind or in front of your two teammates, creating a triangle. That way, if the ball carrier's angle to the near teammate is cut off he will have you as an outlet at a completely different angle.

Fig. 15

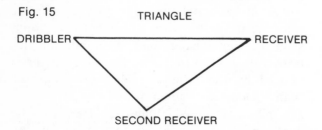

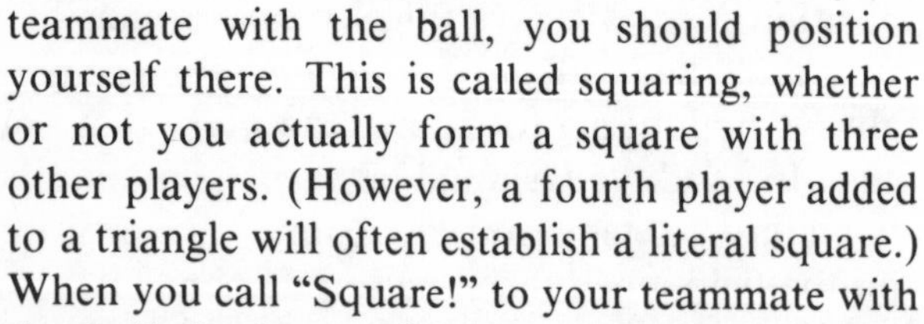

When there is no defender to the side of your teammate with the ball, you should position yourself there. This is called squaring, whether or not you actually form a square with three other players. (However, a fourth player added to a triangle will often establish a literal square.) When you call "Square!" to your teammate with the ball, he knows for sure that he has a free pass if he goes directly lateral in your direction.

Fig. 16

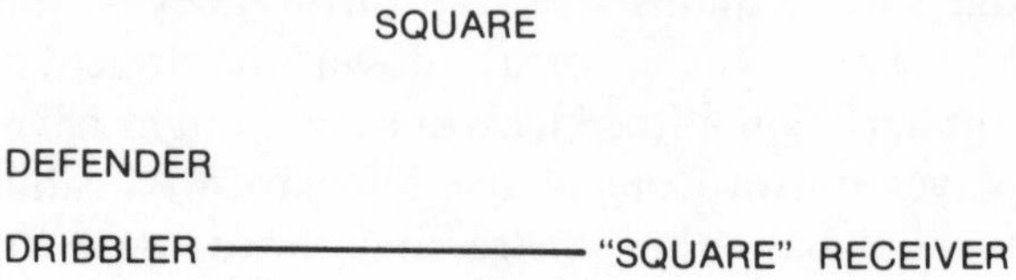

SQUARE

DEFENDER

DRIBBLER ——————————— "SQUARE" RECEIVER

Keeping Subunits Fluid

Again, when traveling in square or triangular units, avoid getting into habits. If each player takes up the same position in such a unit each time that the unit is working, the defense will know what to expect and soon enough will learn how to cope with the strengths and weaknesses of the unit. So shift around—keep your subunit a fluid, kaleidoscopic, unpredictable, kinetic geometry.

To do this, try to incorporate the techniques already mentioned, plus the following kinds of play, which are effective in special situations but cannot constitute a steady style.

1. Develop two-on-one situations whenever you can. You can accomplish this by running to the player with the ball or, if you have the ball, by taking it to a teammate. Often a backward pass will upset the defenders enough to throw them off and generate a two-on-one for you. Two-on-one fast breaks, the most powerful of scoring plays, are created when forwards avoid overinvolving themselves in the defensive play. Eight or nine players ought to be enough to hold any team in the backfield. When you pass to a player, your job is not finished. Follow up the pass, follow the ball, and create a two-on-one. You are much less likely to be closely guarded *after* passing, so that is one of the best times to run off the ball and gain an edge on the defense.

2. Try "flooding" a section of the field from time to time, sending four or five players into an area where there are ordinarily only three. If the defense players stay in their assigned zones, you will have a four- or five-on-three situation in the flooded area. If the defenders mark player to player and move into the flooded area, you have created a wide-open space to which the ball can be passed (to your fullback on the opposite side, for example, coming up on an offensive charge). If you maintain a flood for a while, flooding can shift the expectations of the defense, so that you

An almost infinite variety of possible passing combinations is available to three players in a triangle. How can this defender hope to win the ball?

compel the defense to place an undue number of players on one side of the field. Once you have drawn the defense into that strategy, you will have many opportunities for a fast break to the unflooded side. One way to flood is simply by having your wing play on the inside for a while. Then, when the defense is no longer expecting a touchline run on his side, send him out to the line again for an open pass and an offensive thrust.

3. Don't be afraid to go backward with the ball, except when you are near your own goal, in which case this is a rather dangerous play. At midfield particularly, not every pass is required to penetrate and move forward. The defense will usually expect you to try to push forward all of the time, so that your primarily defensive players will ordinarily be open for a pass. The play backward serves to slow the ball down when it is necessary for your team to set up, and it is also a good way to get the ball to the other side of the field with relative safety. When your own angle for a pass is cut off, that of the player behind you will often be clear and easy. You

sometimes need to take one step backward in order to go two steps forward.

4. Few teams will succeed by using frequent long passes and indiscriminate kicks downfield. But there definitely *is* a place for the long pass, and you should use the long pass when the time is right for it. (*Only* when the time is right, though. Long balls are simply too hard to receive and control to be used as a normal or regular passing mode.) Try to *set up* the moment for a long pass. Try to draw the fullbacks, the last line of the opposing defense, up as far as possible. Then the long ball, over their heads or down the touchline, becomes a gigantic version of the through pass. Your fleet forwards beat the defenders to the ball and drive in for the shot. Long balls often need to be chipped or to have a little backspin put on them so that they will not skid too far from your player or out-of-bounds. The best use of a long pass is as a penetration or to set up a wing. Simply spotting a player upfield is not good enough. He should be relatively free of defenders and in position to get behind the defense. Otherwise his delay in

regaining control of the ball—unless he is a Pele—will give the defense enough time to recover and perhaps to take it from him during the inevitable contest for possession at the moment of reception.

TIPS FROM THE STARS: ADVICE TO A YOUNG PLAYER

Play to enjoy the game of soccer, that's the most important thing. If you're not having fun you won't play well. The game is getting faster and faster, so you should always try to do like the Romans did: Build your roads in a straight line. Work fast, catch the defenders off guard, give the defenders no time to recuperate.

Giorgio Chinaglia

A young player should train as hard as he can. He should concentrate on his weaknesses. When I was young I was weak with my left foot, so I practiced with it all the time. Developing positional sense comes with experience. You've just got to play and play—after a while it comes automatically. It's really an art—you can really use your imagination in soccer.

Peter Silvester

The most common mistakes of young soccer players are: (1) Defenders not guarding their men close enough (one yard is good coverage). (2) Running away from the man with the ball. Players should come and *support* the man with the ball. Come close for close passing. Close passing is where it's at. (3) Ball watching—always keep your man in sight, no matter what else is happening on the field.

Bobby Smith

INNER TEAM MOVEMENT

Much of the success in moving the ball is in the heads of the players, or in the collective head of the team. You need to believe that your team can, collectively, keep control of the ball, and you need to search for the right team rhythm.

Some teams will do best with one-touch play (making the pass at the same instant that the ball is received), some with quick dribbling interspersed with rapid triangulated passes, some by using slow and deliberate ball control and working slowly upfield while the defense players run themselves ragged trying for an interception. But every team must find the rhythm that is right for the players who are on it. You have to try and feel the rhythm, to wait for it, to wait until the feeling is solid and real. Then define what features of your team style work best (for example, lots of fast passes or fewer passes that are set up better) and develop those features. Cultivate the style of moving the ball that enables your team to play rhythmically.

A peculiar aspect of the game of soccer is that a team's *rhythm* is what the team is. Play for the rhythm, not for spectacular moves or even goals. If your team can develop a steady rhythm, everything else will follow. If your team does not learn to work in rhythmic patterns, no amount of strategy or individual skills will help it to win ball games. Think of a rock band that cannot play in rhythm. The band will sound horrible even if the lead guitarist is the world's best. Now a soccer team is not a rock band, to be sure, but the same principle applies.

Watch any great team. You will see that goals are scored when a powerful rhythm is generated. Without rhythm a team is just a sloppy collection of kickers and dribblers. This is one case in which function follows form. When you are able to play with the ball in rhythm, the breakaways follow, the goals follow, the great defense follows. Every group of people who work together must develop a rhythm that will enable them to do their job well, whether they are people on a chain gang or people shooting a movie. Without that rhythm nothing gets done. Work for rhythm, not victory. Rhythm allows you to improvise, like jazz players out on the field. Rhythm *brings* victory, effortlessly, because rhythm is the overpowering force in the universe. You can harness the power of rhythm. Try to think of yourself as a dancer rather than as an athlete. You will find that this helps you to win.

6
Stopping the Ball

Thus far our discussion of soccer has focused on the offensive aspect of the game—passing, receiving, trapping, moving the ball, and so on. But that is, of course, only half the story. An ability to control the ball means very little if you cannot get hold of the ball. Soccer is a game of opposites. For every pass there should be a reception, for every kick a trap, for every player an opposing player, and for every instant in which one team is playing offense, another team must be playing defense.

Defense means three things: preventing your opponents from making the plays they are attempting to make, preventing your opponents from scoring goals, and taking the ball away from your opponents. All three things are really one—*stopping the ball* when you are on defense.

The ball is stopped through a combination of tackling skills, efficient marking of the opposing players, forcing mistakes on their part, and developing an intuitive sense about when to go after the ball and when to leave it alone. What's required in your soccer play is wisdom, not heroics.

Good defense is really a completely different game from ball-control soccer, and you should think of it as a different moment in the sport of soccer. Different, but just as important. Defense is not for the worst players on the team—it's for the best players. Too often in lower-level soccer, it is the worst players who are stuck back to defend the goal—giving the opposing players an easy time of it when they are closing in for a score. Most outstanding teams are built from the defense first, later adding the offense to a strong defense. Although less spectacular, a team's ability to stop the ball is every bit as important as its ability to move the ball.

Let's examine the elements of successful ball stopping.

TACKLING

To play good defensive soccer you must learn how to tackle. There are many kinds of tackling, from a little poke with the foot to a full-blown body slide. But whatever the technique, you should always remember to tackle the ball, not the player. You and your team are trying to get possession of the ball, not to trip your opponents or to force them to the ground. Tackling often becomes an aggressive outlet for unsophisticated players who are used to American football and hunger for body contact. But tackling is not an opportunity to "get rough." It is a technique for taking the ball from the opposing player—no more, no less. So remember, you are tackling the *ball*. Save your hostilities for a boxing ring. On the other hand, you must not be afraid to make contact with the opposing player in order to get the ball. You will never take the ball if you are afraid. Go after the ball, and go after it hard (but don't forget that it is the ball you are after, not some fellow human being's blood).

The tackle is a two-step process. First, you must block the ball, preventing the dribbler from continuing his progress. Then you must take the ball away from the dribbler, gain possession of it. The entire process is performed with the *feet*. You cannot grab the other player, or push him, or throw a block on him, or trip him. Your only tool is your foot, which you use to "grab" the ball. Properly timed (and you only tackle when tackling is *appropriate*), a tackle should win the ball much of the time. Frequently, though, you will serve your basic purpose—stopping your opponent's play—merely by getting a foot on the ball and kicking it away. This is less desirable than gaining control of the ball, but it is surely better than failing to stop your opponent's play at all.

The Front Tackle

The basic idea of the front tackle is to place yourself between the ball carrier and his options for forward movement. Try to get yourself as squarely in front of him as you can. Then reach in with your foot and stop the ball by placing your foot *directly* behind the ball. Merely touching the ball is not sufficient. You have to get enough foot on it to block the dribbler's motion and to overcome the natural momentum that he will have behind the ball when he tries to force it past your block. In most cases, you should try to put your foot against the ball in the same way that you would for a side-of-the-foot pass, blocking it with the full instep.

As you move in on the ball, your weight will be on the planted, nontackling foot. This leaves your tackling foot free to make last-minute adjustments. You'll probably have to, since the opposing player will be trying to avoid your tackle every bit as much as you will be trying to execute it. When you do get your tackling foot on the ball, your weight should be on the nontackling, planted foot, to give you support, leverage, and power. Otherwise the dribbler will force the ball past you and/or knock you over. If you are solidly planted, however, your opponent's own momentum will work against him, and he will go past you or spin away from you. The moment he loses his balance, you should hook the ball with your tackling foot and pull in the direction opposite to his movement, thus gaining possession.

The successful execution of this most basic tackle requires determination—you must stand firm in the face of your opponent's momentum and of his attempts to push the ball past you, and you must keep fighting for the ball even if your opponent momentarily gains the edge. You cannot try and then falter. Once you have committed yourself you must *stay* committed, doing everything in your power to get your foot on the ball. If your opponent moves the ball away from you, go after him and begin your standing tackle again.

A good front tackle also requires good timing. Timing can really be learned only through experience, but you should be aware of the features to look for that determine whether or not your timing is on the mark. You can't just go flying at the player with the ball. Once you've lost control of your weight, your momentum, he will have an easy time faking you out or simply shooting past you. As you enter the tackle, you must approach slowly. Your stance should be a fairly wide one, presenting the broadest possible obstacle to your opponent and providing you with a flexible, stable base from which to launch your move. Get yourself in position quickly. Then slow down, size up the situation, and see whether you can force the dribbler to go in one direction or another by the manner in which you place your body in front of him. Once *he* is committed, then you can commit yourself in a lightning-quick stab into and for the ball. However, if you go for the ball before your opponent has committed himself to a direction and a move, he will lose you. So be both careful and quick as you practice your tackling coordination. Each time you miss, ask yourself what went wrong. Did you strike too fast or too slow? Was your weight properly distributed, or were you off balance? Did you get your foot in front of the ball or merely close to the ball? Don't be afraid to plant your shoulder in such a way as to block your opponent *after* you have made contact with the ball. Don't hesitate once you have encountered the right moment for your stealing operation. It is better to wind up with egg on your face after a good try than to fail because you hesitated, because you could not back up your decision with your whole self and body.

The Sliding Tackle

This is both one of the most spectacular and one of the most useful plays in soccer. Master the sliding tackle, and you will not only stop and steal the ball many times, you will also thoroughly intimidate your opponents. An intimidated team is like a neurotic individual—it will never reach its potential, it will never act with confidence, decisiveness, style, and flair. If you can shake up the minds of your opponents you will not have to worry very much about their feet.

Sliding will often get you to a ball that you could not have reached by running, because it saves you the motion of that extra step. Too, your outstretched leg can actually reach a few inches farther than it could if you remained standing. But of course timing is crucial for the sliding tackle. Miss this one, and you are out of the play altogether. Still, the sliding tackle will help you break up plays, gain the ball, get the ball out of danger when necessary, save balls that would otherwise go out-of-bounds, and pick off passes that you would not ordinarily be able to reach. You will use sliding tackles to stop a dribbler with the ball, but sliding tackles are also useful when you are trying to capture only the ball itself, even if there is no opponent against you.

Sliding tackles are usually made when you are approaching the opponent somewhat from the side. You *cannot make a sliding tackle from the rear of an opponent and brush his legs*—that is a violation of the rules. You can only slide from the side or the front, and you must tackle the ball, not the player. If you miss the ball and trip your opponent you are liable to have a foul called against you. A free kick will be awarded the other team, so that if the foul has been committed near your own goal, you have really created a troublesome situation. But if you make contact with the ball first, it is up to your opponent to avoid your legs. So proper timing and aim are critical here.

To execute a sliding tackle you must focus all of your consciousness on the ball. You take a risk in this play—if it's successful, you're a hero; if it fails because you slid too early or too late or missed the ball, you're a goat. As the opponent dribbling the ball approaches your area, run hard so that you are slightly in front of him. Try to gear your approach to force him to the outside of the field if possible—if you succeed, there's less room for him to maneuver or get off a dangerous pass. Then time your slide so that you will contact the ball before your opponent can touch it away from you. That means that you must slide *in between* his steps, on the half step, as it were. Swing your foot into the ball, throwing your leg as if it were a spear.

You will go down on the ground on the *opposite* leg and side from that which you have aimed at the ball (that is, if you go for the tackle with your right foot, you will slide on your left leg and side). The slide is no different from a slide to the base in baseball (and the reason for making the slide is the same—extra reach with your sliding leg). If the slide is performed in this way, your foot will *hook* the ball, you will make contact with your instep. (As you slide you may also want to brace yourself with the hand that is on the side on which you are sliding—the left hand in the above example.)

When you make a sliding tackle you really have to meet the ball solidly. You can't just touch it, you have to make it *go* somewhere. You can send it out-of-bounds if you are near the touchline, or you can try to use the tackle to make a pass to one of your teammates. But whatever you do, make sure that you get the ball far away from your opponent. For you will now be on the ground and unable to defend against him if he should regain possession of the ball. That leaves him free and your team one player short.

Be sure that your tackle is a strong one. Your muscles should be tensed (although you *do* have to be relaxed when you slide), and your leg should be bent slightly at the knee so that you can come in on the ball with a kicking motion. A strong tackle will give you a great psychological advantage over your opponent—if he loses the ball and is upended when you tackle, he will become insecure when trying to dribble against you. Once you have removed the ball from his possession, rise up quickly and send it to one of your teammates. Make your opponent afraid of your skills—the less able he is to concentrate when you are near, the less able he will be to play the ball accurately and effectively.

An important point, often overlooked, is that your foot should contact the ball in the middle or slightly on top. This gives you a good "back-stopping" effect and tends to counterbalance your opponent's already existing momentum. If your foot is low on the ball, he is likely to push the ball over your foot and past you. So re-

member, come in strong, slide on the leg opposite the one that is reaching in, work on accurate timing, get your foot directly behind the ball, and tackle the ball, not the player. The sliding tackle should be used sparingly, only when the time is right. However, when the time is right and the execution is right, a sliding tackle will save many a dangerous defensive moment. The sliding tackle can also be used to keep the ball from going out-of-bounds, converting a corner kick, for example, into a much less harmful throw-in.

When is the time right for a sliding tackle? This is basically a cat-and-mouse situation, in which you slide at the ball *only when the opposing player has less than full control*. If the opposing player has firm possession of the ball, your tackle will usually do little more than take you out of the play. You should be guarding your opponent closely on defense, so closely that he does not have time to really gain good control of the ball upon receiving a pass. When the pass comes to him, he will be busy trying to bring it under control. This is an excellent time to come in for a sliding tackle. Make your tackle at the first chance you get—take advantage of your opponent's uncertain equilibrium

Here the tackler has gone down with good form—sliding on his nontackling leg, bracing himself with the arm on the same side, reaching in with his tackling foot. But guess who's going to come up with the ball? Meanwhile, the tackler's slide has taken him out of the play.

In this variation of the sliding tackle, the tackler goes in on his knee but remains upright, which is often more effective. Even if the tackler misses, he can still recover quickly. The slide saves a step, perhaps just that fraction of a second necessary to reach the ball. Note that the tackler comes in at right angles to try and wrest the ball away. If you come in straight on you must overcome the ball handler's momentum (above). This is a good tackle for any situation, but for wet fields in particular. The tackler's body is placed to force the ball handler to move in a specific direction. Then the tackler goes in with his foot, remaining upright and ready to recover should he miss. The tackler's foot must be placed very squarely behind the ball to overcome the ball handler's moving weight (below).

If you can, stay on your feet when tackling. Here the ball handler has gone down and the tackler, because he has remained upright and in control, is ready to pass down to his waiting teammate.

as he receives the ball, and move in on him right away, the instant he touches the ball.

If your opponent already has good control, you cannot just go in flying. You must dog him closely, keeping yourself between your opponent and the goal, and forcing your opponent to the outside if you can. Give your opponent as little room to work as possible, without leaving yourself vulnerable to a fast breakaway run on his part. Try to position yourself so that the available spaces to which he can go are limited, thus giving yourself some measure of predictability. Now, while you are dogging him you wait for him to make a mistake—to kick the ball just a little too far in front on his dribble, or perhaps to hesitate and stop the ball because you have blocked his passage. Then you make your move, sliding into the ball forcefully and with determination. But beware of having too quick a trigger. If your opponent is definitely in possession of the ball, you *must* wait for a mistake that gives you access. If you don't, you'll slide into nothingness. First, force the error, then steal the ball. But don't think that you are so agile that you can step right in and take the ball

when your opponent has tight control. He won't let you. Pressure him, force him to the touchline, where he will panic. When your opponent has lost his cool, he will lose the ball.

TIPS FROM THE STARS: TACKLING

Tackling—proper positioning of your body is the key. You don't just tackle with a leg or foot, you get your whole body behind the ball. Be sure you have a chance to come up with the ball, don't just tackle out of desperation. You need a keen sense of timing. Use the inside part of your foot for tackling. A sliding tackle is not used for possession, it's for breaking up a play.

Al Trost

The Shoulder Charge

As you are dogging the opponent with the ball, you can sometimes force mistakes on his part, or even gain possession, through the use of the shoulder charge. This is one of the few permissible forms of direct physical contact in soccer, but if it is not executed properly, you will be called for a foul.

In the shoulder charge you push your opponent off the ball with your shoulder. You are permitted to use *only* your shoulder, *not* your elbows or your hands. You cannot charge with your shoulder from behind your opponent, and you can only use the shoulder charge if you actually have a chance at getting the ball.

When running alongside your opponent (if he has possession of the ball), you can attempt to gain better position by pushing him off to the side with your shoulder (the best way is to push against his shoulder). Only the shoulder can make contact—you can't use, for example, your hips or your thighs. You should only "charge" your opponent enough to throw him off the ball and to give yourself access to it. If you are too rough with this play, you will be called for a foul and your opponent will be awarded a free kick.

You can use the shoulder charge to force your opponent to the touchline, where he has little room to maneuver. At that point you might find that you have created a situation in which you can make a standing or sliding tackle and take the ball away, or stop the play by kicking it out-of-bounds. The shoulder charge is a valuable weapon in your arsenal of defensive tricks, whether you are a fullback or a center forward, but you should always remember that it cannot be an excuse to throw a cross-body block or to get rough simply for the sake of getting rough. It is only legal as a sincere attempt to gain control of the ball and in no other circumstances.

THE DEFENSIVE STANCE

Your effectiveness at stopping the ball will often depend, as it were, on how you start your stopping. A proper defensive stance—one from which you can move quickly in any direction and one which helps you to avoid being faked out by your opponents—is a necessary tool for

This is a legal shoulder charge. In making a shoulder charge, be sure to keep your arms in so that you don't foul your opponent.

any soccer player. Often a good stance is all you need to play good defense, enabling you to dispense with tackles, charges, and the like. If the offensive player cannot go around you, cannot get behind you, cannot "beat" you, you have rendered him harmless.

When you mark an opponent, your legs should be about two feet apart, your knees should be slightly bent, and your arms should be held out from your body. From this position you can move quickly to the left or to the right and forward or back. Stay on your toes—if you remain flat-footed, it will take longer for you to move. Keeping your legs spread will enable you to throw your weight to another space rapidly, but you must guard against having the opposing player push the ball through the space between your legs. Stay in a semicrouch. It's easier to move from a low position. Practice jumping left and right from this wide, low stance, without crossing one leg in front of the other.

You'll see that if you stay low and wide, the opposing dribbler will have a difficult time getting past you or faking you out. If you merely stand up straight, your center of gravity is too high and you're an easy target for a fake. But if you maintain the proper defensive stance, the opposing dribbler will be forced to slow down his play because he will not see any way around you. Often the stance alone becomes your prime defensive tactic, for slowing down your opponent, forcing him to make mistakes when he doesn't see an easy opening, is what defense is all about.

Keep yourself between the ball and the goal. This is a basic rule of obvious import. By positioning yourself in this way, you prevent your opponent from making a shot or a dribbling breakaway, and you make that most dangerous of plays, the penetrating pass, extremely difficult to execute. If possible, you should try to angle yourself against your opponent to keep him both away from the goal *and* trending toward the touchline. Push your opponent toward the out-of-bounds—that's the safest area on the field, giving him the least room for maneuvering, and in that area you can often break up a play simply by reaching in and kicking the ball out.

Remember to use the defensive stance to dog your opponent and force him to make a mistake. Only when he does can you commit yourself to a tackle to break up the play or steal the ball. Stay light and alert, and watch the *ball*, not the fakes of your opponent's body or head, or even of his feet. Only by watching the *ball* will you know where it is going. Focus all of your attention on that bit of pressurized space. When the opportunity presents itself, strike like lightning to make that pressurized space your own. But never make a move for the ball unless the opportunity is *there*. On defense, your major role, whether you are guarding a dribbler or a free player, is to stay on the play and to avoid the deception that the opposition will constantly be trying to practice on you.

DEFENSIVE STYLES AND REACTIVE INTELLIGENCE

In our treatment of alignments and tactics (Chapter 8) we will deal with specific kinds of defensive team play. Before putting it all together, though, it's necessary to break down the components and the forms of defensive soccer, for these will reappear again and again in all of the various tactics. Defense, as we have begun to see already, is far more than merely running to the player with the ball and trying to take the ball away from him.

The ideal style of defensive play is one in which the opposing player is prevented from getting the ball in the first place. In order to accomplish this, the players of the defense team should mark tightly all of the players of the opposing team, anticipate the passes of the opposing team, and dog the dribbler steadily, without being taken out of the play. You and your team should work toward *closing off all of the passing outlets on the field*. The more your team can compel the opposing team to dribble, the more often your team will come up with the ball and the slower will be the opposing team's movement of the ball.

Zonal Marking

Among the best international teams today, the currently favored system of marking is a zonal one. Each defender covers a predetermined zone and marks any attacking players who enter his zone. But zone play cannot be a rigid and mechanical "knee-jerk" system. Zones must overlap, and defenders must *always support* one another. If one defender finds himself with a zone that has been flooded by attackers, his teammates must come to help him out. Or if a defender commits himself to a tackle or goes up for a risky head, his teammates must come to back him up. Good defense requires the team members to follow their assignments rigorously and, just as rigorously, to abandon their assignments in order to provide support for a teammate. If either ingredient is missing—covering a zone or providing support—a defense will become porous and it will collapse.

Take a look at the map of fullback defensive zones. We are using fullbacks in our example, but there are zones all over the field to be covered by halfs and even strikers (when the need for total defensive pressure is great). There are also many different possible configurations of zones, depending on the particular strategy and system that a team decides to use.

It is generally agreed that four fullbacks are sufficient to cover the entire width of the field in front of the goal area, and today most teams use a line of four fullbacks or some close variant of the "back four." One-fourth of the field width, approximately twenty-five yards, is not too much for one player to cover, and in most cases attackers will spread themselves sufficiently (to free themselves to take passes and work the ball around) so that only one or two attackers will occupy a zone at any given time. The fullback's responsibility is to pick up any player who enters the zone and to mark him player-to-player. But the matter is not quite so simple as that, and a zonal defender must above all not think of himself as an animal in a cage who cannot leave his "assigned" zone.

At some times a fullback will be marking the ball carrier who moves across one zone and into another. Obviously the fullback cannot stop at the boundary of his zone and let the dribbler go. At other times a fullback's own zone will be free of attackers, but the neighboring fullback will be outmanned by two or more forwards. At such times the fullback has to slide over and help out. Zonal play must be flexible and fluid, just like the rest of soccer.

Fullbacks (and anyone else playing defense) must learn to pass off attackers to each other. When an opposing player cuts for a pass, for

Fig. 17. Fullback defensive zones.

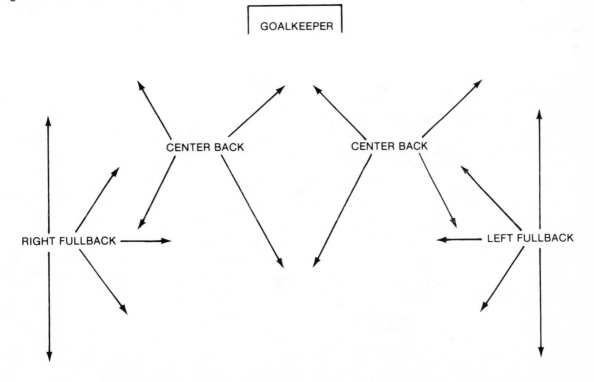

example, the fullback who had *not* been marking him may now be in a much better defensive position than the fullback who had been marking him. Both fullbacks must see this, and call out to each other, and the marking fullback should allow the striker to slide off while the next fullback picks him up. But it must be *clear* to both fullbacks that this is the appropriate move; otherwise the striker will slide off with no one to guard him. Once the attacker has been passed off, the formerly marking fullback cannot just stand there twiddling his shorts. He must quickly look for another opposing player to guard, and he must be alert to any situation in which he may have to back up, to *support,* the newly marking fullback.

It should be clear by now that a zone defense does not provide a clear-cut pattern of responsibilities for defenders, although it does provide a basic pattern. You cannot safely say to yourself, for example, "My mission is to guard the right-hand defensive quadrant of the field." Soccer is too fluid, and things are never that simple. Your area is a general one. Your real mission is to guard *players,* not real estate. Though you cannot give an opposing team too much unoccupied space in any zone, at the same time you cannot afford to remain in your zone if there is no opposing player for you to guard. If you do, your team will have only ten players instead of eleven—while you wait for the play to come to your zone.

We have used fullbacks in our example. But the example holds just as true for midfielders and strikers. Patrol your zone like a lion guarding its den, but when you are not needed in your zone, move to a neighboring zone where you *are* needed. You should always remember, however, that your zone is then unmanned. You should return to your zone as soon as possible, and in the event that the play goes to your zone, it is your responsibility to return immediately. When you move away from your zone, take stock of the location of all opposing players. Be aware of the players who might run into your zone for a pass, and keep tabs on them out of the corner of your eye. Astute offensive teams will often try to draw a defender out of his zone by flooding a

Tight marking means staying with your opponent like a shadow. When marking, watch your opponent, not the ball.

nearby zone. Then they quickly send a player into the vacated area for an unchallenged pass, with clear sailing ahead of him. As you play your zone, worry about more than the mere zone. Worry about the tactics of the other side. Ask yourself what the other side is up to, what its true strategy is. Once you get a good fix on your opponents' style of play, once you can predict with some accuracy what they will do with the ball, you can then know with confidence how free you are to improvise with your zone. Tuning in to the offensive patterns in this way will also help you to intercept many a pass, since most teams tend to fall into habitual types of passing and ball movement.

Now that you are in your zone and marking a player, what, exactly, should you be doing? The answer to that question, like the answer to any soccer question, is part physical and part mental.

Making Your Presence Felt

The first and most obvious rule of marking is to stay close to your opponent. Your first priority is to *make your presence felt*. This even takes precedence over being in position to stop your opponent should he get the ball or to intercept a pass that may come to him. The psychological importance of your presence is just as crucial as your strategic location. The player you are marking should *know* that you are near. He should feel afraid, afraid that if he receives the ball you will be all over him and that he will have no time to bring the ball under control. Your opponent should be insecure; he should lack confidence; he should feel that he is likely to lose the ball to you when it comes; his necessary quality of coolheadedness should be cut to the barest possible minimum.

And beyond that, the player who has the ball should be aware that you are closely guarding his teammate. He should feel afraid to pass the ball to the teammate covered by your defensive play. That will make the ball carrier hold the ball longer than he should, render him vulnerable to a tackle from your teammates, cause him to pass with insecurity or to dribble the ball too long and lose it to your team. The first goal of defense is to force the other team into mistakes,

mistakes of dribbling, passing, and judgment. When the ball carrier looks over to the player you are marking, he should see an enemy shirt guarding his teammate, *your* enemy shirt. He will be reluctant, then, to pass the ball to that teammate. If all of your teammates are guarding similarly, the ball carrier will become panicky, because he will have no passing outlet. He will be forced to stop, or to make a dribbling or passing mistake. This will give your team an opportunity to take possession of the ball, an opportunity that you have created.

When the ball is in your defensive half of the field, you will in most cases position yourself alongside your opponent. Keep him to the outside of the field, to the side nearest to the touchline. That way, if he does get the ball, he will have to go outside with it, and will be unable to take the more dangerous interior route which can bring him in front of your goal.

You stand alongside your opponent rather than behind him in order to get the offside rule working in your favor. If your opponent is behind you and the pass comes forward, he will be called for offsides if there is no *other* defender between him and the goal. Of course, you must be careful if you stand alongside your opponent. If he is fast, you are vulnerable to his run down the field or to a chipped through pass over your head. But by standing alongside your opponent, you force him to remain farther from your goal than he would like to be, you "pull" him offside. Be sure, though, that none of your teammates are back behind you. Otherwise you cannot make your opponent go offside, and he can go behind you with impunity.

If you are closer to midfield, or if teammates are behind you, you should position yourself slightly *behind* the opponent you are marking. You should be close enough to come in and contest the ball if a pass comes to him, but behind him so that he cannot make forward progress if he does get the ball. One yard is a good distance.

Anticipation

When you are marking a player (one who does not have possession of the ball), you must watch not only your player but also the total course and configuration of the play. This will help you with a key aspect of defense: *anticipating* the movement of the attacking team and of the player you are guarding. Often that player will try to cut quickly into an open space to receive a pass or to shake you off. You must watch where your opponents are taking the ball, and you must watch the field, always remaining aware of the open spaces as they develop, so that you can *anticipate* where your player might go. Sometimes it will be imperative that you follow him; sometimes you will be better off remaining in your zone to pick up a new attacker who enters it. Which course you take is always a matter of judgment, but you will have no basis for judgment unless you are aware of the total picture of play on the field.

This awareness tells you not only where to move, it also tells you when to commit yourself. As should be clear by now, the basic mode of defense in soccer is *containment*. You and your team try to contain the play of your opponents, preventing them from working the ball the way they want to and forcing them into mistakes which become opportunities for you. You don't just dive in willy-nilly and attempt to steal the ball away.

Containment and Commitment

But there is a time for containment and a time for commitment. When you can effectively *anticipate* the opposition's play, *or* when—by means of your containment strategies—you can force your opponents to make a mistake, you create moments in which the right course of action is to *commit* yourself to taking possession of the ball.

If you are standing next to your opponent (or slightly behind him), and you have a total awareness of his possible movements and the ball carrier's passing options, you are sooner or later going to pick up on an offensive move *before* it happens. You are going to see, for example, that the ball carrier is trapped, that he can only pass to the player you are guarding. Or even if he is not trapped, you may see through a flicker of his eyes or some other signal that the pass is going to come to your player. This is the genesis of an interception. If you can "see" a play developing ahead of time, if you can receive a "telegraph message" because of your own and your teammates' tight defensive play, then you can take the risk of *committing* yourself.

Jump out in front of your player and cut off

Containing your player means staying in front of him, giving him no room to work, slowing him down. Stopping your player is just as effective as taking the ball away from him. The defender must watch the ball, not the ball handler—the ball can't fake.

Pele contains his players from the low, basic position. He is ready to move in any direction. See how Pele watches the ball, not the player.

the pass that you have "seen" coming. Go ahead and commit yourself to the ball. If you have been able to see a pass coming and can get to it, that pass was a mistake forced by your team's total defense. Let one of your teammates worry about covering for you in the event that you fail to intercept, or yell "Cover!" to your nearest teammate. Go for the ball with every ounce of effort in your body. This is the chance that you and your defense have been waiting for. Defense is not all passive and containing—it can also become aggressive and committed, and the best way to make the switch is by cutting off an anticipated pass.

Similar situations can arise if you are marking the player with the ball. As we have discussed, the general way of guarding the player with the ball is to contain him—to dog him, to cut off his passing angles, to force him to the outside, to stay so close to him that it's difficult for him to move the ball fast, yet far enough away from him to prevent him from breaking

free of you. You contain your opponent, and you try to force him to make a mistake. Then, when he does (perhaps by kicking the ball too far for control or by stopping the ball inadvertently), you move in aggressively for your tackle.

Anticipation and total awareness of the field play the same role in determining your moment for a defensive strike when you are guarding the player who *does* have the ball as they do when you are guarding a player who does not have the ball. Be aware of the location of all attacking players. Know what the ball carrier *might* do with the ball, whether it be a pass to an open teammate or a move to an open space. If you maintain this awareness you will be able to anticipate the ball carrier's move—especially if his options are limited—and cut him off when he makes it. If you have forced the ball carrier into the corner of the field at your end, for example, he can only go directly toward the goal or backward. If the teammate behind him is marked by one of your defenders, you know that he can only go toward the goal. With this advantage you are able to position yourself in his path, the only path he has, and commit yourself to a tackle, knowing where the ball must be. Since he has no place to go, you close in slowly, in a careful defensive stance, and when you are close enough you go directly for the ball. Awareness and anticipation always give you the edge on defense.

Defensive Support

There is a third crucial ingredient to effective defense, to successfully stopping the ball, and that is support. When one of your teammates has been maneuvered into a situation in which he is forced to guard two players—one of whom may have the ball—don't just stand there and watch him. *Run to his aid.* The player you leave unguarded in doing so is not nearly as dangerous as the interpassing that can occur against your teammate when the ball carrier *and another player* are against him. Go in there and break up the play, just as you would go to an open space to create a passing outlet on offense. At other times, a nearby teammate may be caught in a tight, difficult, or risky play. If he has to go up for a head on a long ball, don't just watch him make the play. He might miss, you know. Go around behind him as a backup, ready to pick up the ball if he does miss. If a nearby teammate should gain possession of the ball and begin to bring it upfield into your team's territory, quickly run to give him a passing outlet, behind or to the side. Forget about the player you have been marking. Your team is now on the offense, and your teammate needs support. Be sure to call out to him, so that he knows where you are and that you are clear. Never make the fatal mistake of so many beginners who call for the ball when they are *not* clear. Support is not support unless you can actually give it.

If the goalie has come out for a save and is in a scuffle for the ball, look to see whether you can give him support by moving into the goal to head or kick out a possible shot. If the opponent you are marking is not really part of the play, you are going to help your team much more by supporting your goalkeeper than by mechanically sticking to your defensive assignment.

Beating the Other Team to the Ball

Whether on offense or on defense, this factor, which might well be called the "hustle factor," is often decisive in determining the final score. The fact that your basic attitude on defense is one of containment should not prevent you from going all out to pick up any pass that you can reach and especially to gain control of loose (uncontrolled) balls. The team that picks up the most loose balls, particularly in its own territory, will usually be the team that wins the match. To pick up loose balls you must be hustling all the time. You can't let your opponent have the ball without a fight. You must move aggressively for the ball, fearlessly and with confidence, and you must get to it first. When you beat your opponents to the ball you beat them physically and psychologically, and both types of victory are necessary for consistent winning soccer. Through anticipation and awareness, and the willingness to abandon containment for commitment when the time is right, you will find your team controlling the game—especially at midfield—and executing many goal-scoring fast breaks that would otherwise never have come into existence.

Remember, *the team starts with defense,* with stopping the opposition. When your team cannot be scored upon, it cannot be beaten. Wild ball-stealing tactics are not the path to successful defense. But hustle for loose balls. Anticipation, awareness, support, containment, and then—at the right moment—commitment most certainly will stop the opposing attack in its tracks. Many an inferior team has beaten a more experienced and skilled team simply by refusing to grant the other team any momentum or any chances to score.

TIPS FROM THE STARS: STOPPING YOUR MAN

Why do I play good defense? There's no way my man is going to beat me. The absolute first part of your game on defense is stopping your man. Ideally, you should mark your man so tightly that he never gets the ball and you never *have* to stop him. Worry your man, worry whoever might pass to him. If your man is always covered, his teammates will never pass to him, you've taken him out of the ball game. A defensive player can play a great game without ever touching the ball or making a tackle—just by marking his man closely and forcing the attack to change its tactics. Be aggressive, anticipating, always one step ahead—*mark your man right out of the game*. You've got to win the one-on-one battles.

Bobby Smith

7
Set Plays

Though soccer is generally a fluid game of constant action, there are moments when the ball is stopped and the play starts over, as it were, from scratch. These moments—free kicks, throw-ins, goal kicks, and so on—can be used by your team to tremendous advantage. All too few teams plan how to use these "setup" plays, even though a proper execution can often lead to goal-scoring opportunities. You and your team should *never* merely put the ball back in play. You should always attempt a strategic maneuver to milk the greatest possibilities from situations in which you are playing from a stopped ball.

Conversely, when you are on defense you should always know exactly where to play in order to guard *against* the opposition's strategic use of a set play. Each player should know whom to guard on a throw-in, where to stand for a blocking wall, what potentially dangerous moves the offensive team might make.

For both teams, then, set plays provide an opportunity, one of the rare opportunities in soccer, to conduct an organized, planned, predetermined method of teamwork. Set plays can make the difference between winning and losing, and going into a game with a definite set-piece strategy is extremely important to any successful team.

THE WALL

There are only a few ways to set up a wall, but there are many ways for the offensive team to get around it. Learn the basic principles for getting past a wall, and then use your imagination to set up plays that will work against any kind of situation that you may encounter.

The defensive team will often set up a wall if a *free kick* (direct or indirect) has been awarded to the offensive team and the ball is placed within shooting distance of the goal. The purpose of the wall is to block off part of the goalmouth from the shooter—the player taking the free kick—and thus allowing the goalkeeper to patrol considerably less territory. Walls are usually composed of three or four players standing shoulder to shoulder, ten yards or more from the ball (that is a rule).

The wall should always be the minimum distance from the ball—ten yards—since that functions to cut off the maximum angle to the goal.

In addition, other defensive players should mark each attacker who is in any way dangerous. As we shall see, the wall limits only the player behind the ball—the shooter. It is rendered impotent if the shooter passes the ball off to a teammate who is not blocked by the wall. If that happens, the wall should, of course, disband immediately, and its members should revert to standard defensive play.

Wall members should stand with their hands behind their backs—this is to prevent a hands foul in what is a most likely penalty area. A hands foul would lead to a penalty kick, a direct free kick which only the goalie is permitted to defend against. Each player should have his shoulder up next to that of the player beside him. Too, each player should stand with legs slightly spread. The whole point of the wall is to present an impenetrable barrier to the ball (or at least as impenetrable a barrier as the odd shapes of human bodies can create). If a player has his legs too far apart, or if there is a space between two players, the goalie should call out to his teammates and correct the situation. All of this must happen very quickly, for a smart offensive team will take its free kick as fast as it can.

TIPS FROM THE STARS: SETTING UP A WALL

A wall must be planned out in advance. If the ball is directly in front of the goal, you might have five or even six men in the wall; if the angle is sharp, you might have only three. The wall covers up one corner of the goal, and the keeper covers the other. The *midfielder* should stand in front of the goal and position it from the shooter's angle (the goalie no longer does the positioning). Be sure that at least one man is on the wall and *outside the near post* so that the shot can't be bent to the goal around the *outside* of the wall.

Alan Mayer and Arnold Mausser

Offensive and Defensive Free-Kick Play

On defense, in a wall versus free-kick situation, your team's task is to create a barrier, to mark the players other than the player behind the ball, to guard against the attack's strategy of avoiding your wall, and to reform into a tight defense once the free kick has been made. On offense, as you might expect, your team's tasks are quite the opposite.

The offensive team in a free-kick situation will succeed by guile. This is one of the moments in soccer when *intelligence*—a *clever* play properly executed—is the deciding factor. You can try to blast the ball through the blocking wall—it's a valid tactic, and sometimes it will work (we'll discuss the best ways to try that)—but how much easier it is to go around or over a wall! Avoiding the wall, or tricking its members into disbanding, is the best way to take advantage of your free kicks. Here, as in so many other spheres, the smart, carefully considered method turns out to be *more* effective than the mindless exercise of brute strength.

If your name is Pele, you may be able to shoot a curving ball around a wall or a diving ball right over the top of one, but if you are a mere mortal you are going to have to work a play with your teammates to deal with the wall. In most cases the well-planned play will go *around* the wall with at least one, and possibly several, passes. If you do not attempt a tactical maneuver for your free kick, you are simply wasting a key opportunity.

There are many ways to go around a wall. The number open to you depends upon your creativity and imagination (and to some extent upon the configuration that the defense sets up). You should *surprise* the other team, either by coming very fast or by using diversionary tactics. Your plays should be as simple as possible so that they do not get fudged in the execution. They must be well organized—every player must know his role under any circumstances. And, it goes without saying, the plays must be practiced over and over so that in a game situation they are executed perfectly. The best play is worthless if the receiver is unsure of what to do when he gets his pass, or if the passer has not learned, *before* the game, just where and how fast his pass should go.

Always try to set up and start your play quickly. Defenses tend to get confused when they are setting up a wall, and the very physical

Pele sends his kick bending
around the wall.

act of lining up correctly takes time. If the first player is wrongly placed, the whole wall may be off, and you will want to get your play going before the goalie or midfielder has a chance to correct and realign his teammates. Confusion and disequilibrium in the defense are your best allies.

Options of Multiple "Kickers"

It's often a good idea to start your play with two or even three players behind the ball, any one of whom might turn out to be the "kicker." This initiates your deceptions. Let's call the players behind the ball A, B, and C. As potential kickers, they will very likely be unmarked by the defense, which is worried about the area goalward. Even if these players are marked, they are able to break and run, with the element of surprise about where they are going, so that these players can be considered essentially free for attack no matter how the defense is set up.

Many options are open to these three players. Player A might run over the ball and cut to the side of the wall to receive a pass from player B, who has followed him to the ball. B might be open to shoot, or he might backheel the ball to C, who has come up behind him, and let C take the shot. Or B might run right up to the wall,

turn unmarked, and receive a pass from A, then flip the ball out to C, who has run wide of the wall.

A and B could conduct a mock conversation near the ball, as if to decide who will kick it. Meanwhile C sneaks off slightly to the side, just enough to give him a clear shot on goal, unblocked by the wall. Still talking, A or B flips the ball out to C, who takes a fast shot.

Another player, D, might stand right next to the outside member of the defensive wall. There will usually be a space between that member and the next defender. If a pass is sent to D, he could quickly one-touch it to A, B, or C, who is running past him into that space.

Or A might pass the ball to C, who is standing near the wall but not right at it. C then executes a through pass to D, who has run for the goal at the moment of A's pass.

If your players are set up properly, one player can run and call for the ball at one side of the wall, creating a distraction, while in fact the play is going to the other side of the wall.

You can bunch up all of your strikers at the wall and then have them "explode" outward at a predetermined signal, filling the strike zone like shotgun pellets, creating confusion, while a pass or a series of passes go to the prearranged shooter.

Fig. 18. Some ways to get around the wall.

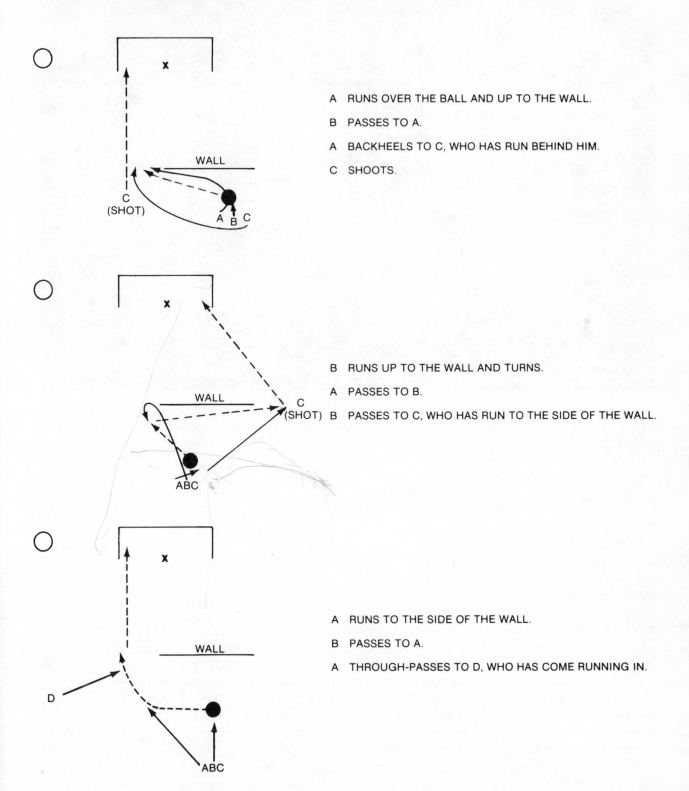

A RUNS OVER THE BALL AND UP TO THE WALL.

B PASSES TO A.

A BACKHEELS TO C, WHO HAS RUN BEHIND HIM.

C SHOOTS.

B RUNS UP TO THE WALL AND TURNS.

A PASSES TO B.

B PASSES TO C, WHO HAS RUN TO THE SIDE OF THE WALL.

A RUNS TO THE SIDE OF THE WALL.

B PASSES TO A.

A THROUGH-PASSES TO D, WHO HAS COME RUNNING IN.

This wall for a corner or direct kick has just broken, and the offensive player in the wall now breaks outside it, unobserved by his opponents. There is open space behind the wall to which he can run for a pass.

It should be apparent that you can go around a wall in an infinite number of ways. Your methods are not limited to skillful interpassing or to fast cuts into a free space. You have every possible psychological tactic at your disposal, too. Free kicks can be an occasion for high drama. That's as much a part of the game of soccer as of any physical skill. If you want to stage a mock argument, or pretend to tie your shoe, go right ahead. It's legal, and it can work wonders. Remember, you are always trying to throw the defense off guard. If you can think of a good trick, use it. There's no reason to be somber and just play "straight" soccer. Many of the best international teams in the history of soccer have won important matches through dramatic tactics that threw the defense off just enough to permit them to score. Subtlety and cunning must be part of your soccer battle plan.

Malcolm Allison, the manager of the great English team Manchester City, stated his free-kick philosophy thus: "Deception, disguise, false running, general hustle and bustle will hide the most obvious plans. Attackers have the advantage. They are bound to be moving first. Defenders must be moving more slowly. Think about it."

Over or through the Wall

On occasion, you may want to try going *over* or *through* the wall. If the defense is looking for your customary pass play, this more direct approach will also have the advantage of surprise. It will keep the defense guessing about your free-kick tactics, and it will keep the wall members insecure, glued to their places. When the free kick is from close range, the most efficient use of your free-kick opportunity may well be to go directly for goal if you have a good shooter or to chip over the wall if you have a good chipper.

The classic method of going *through* the wall is to insert one of your own players into the wall in order to break up its homogeneity and to provide a space for your team at the instant of shooting. Your player might insert himself at the edge or in the middle of the wall, whichever is most advantageous for the shooter. When the shot is taken, the offensive player in the wall ducks or jumps sideways. That leaves a gap through which the ball flies and, hopefully, enters the nets. The goalie's vision is blocked by the offensive player in the wall before he moves aside, the direction of the shot is unexpected, and no defender will be able to stop it.

Good timing is what makes this play work. Your teammate should join or attach himself to the wall *just before* you are about to kick. If he moves in too soon, the defense will be able to compensate for his presence. If he moves in too late, the tactic becomes meaningless. All of this indicates that the attaching player should attach himself as soon as the wall forms and that the kick should be made *immediately* thereafter. The player-in-the-wall *must be sure to get out of the way,* and the kicker must have an accurate foot, capable of putting the ball directly into the hole created by his helper.

Another "twist" on this play is to kick a bent ball. Perhaps the hole made by your player-in-the-wall is not far enough away from the goalie's reach if the shot is straight on. The hole can still provide a passageway for a ball that bends out and up or out and down to a corner of the goal. If you have a kicker with a good bent ball, you can position your wall player with a bent kick in mind from the outset. The wall player may look harmless—perhaps he is standing right in front of the goalie—when in fact he is creating an opening for a shot that is intended for a place quite different from the obvious line a straight kick would take.

Another variant that can work very well and has been used with great success by world class teams is chipping the ball *over* the defensive wall. (Review how to chip in Chapter 3.) You can kick the ball in a standard chip with lots of backspin. But an equally effective way of getting the ball over the wall is to scoop under it with your toe and flick it up (without an actual "impact" kick). Of course, much practice is required to develop good control, but this will float the ball up and over at a nice, slow pace so that your strikers can run up to it for the shot.

The players who are off the ball should position themselves so that they can meet it close to the goal. The moment that the kicker makes contact, they must run in at full speed to meet the ball and shoot. The shot need not be with the foot—it may be, and often will be, a header. Too, the onrushing striker can add still another fillip by passing the ball to a teammate on the other side of the goal (or anywhere a teammate is free) for an even clearer shot. The chip itself need not be intended to fall in front of or near the goal. It can be directed to an open space where a teammate can easily take control behind the wall (this play might be to a wing, for example). The point is to get the ball over and behind the wall. The shot might come on the third or even the fourth offensive touch. That doesn't matter. What matters is that your attacking team have possession in that very explosive area near the goal.

Sometimes the goalie will be well out of the goal for a free kick that is placed at the side of the field and is seemingly far off. In this case you might want to try a chip over both the wall *and* the goalie, aiming directly for the goal (you can do this only if the kick is a "direct" kick—see the rules in Chapter 10). It is extremely difficult for a goalie to field a ball that is floating over his head, and your teammates at the far post may be able to polish off the goal even if your chip does not take the ball into the nets.

The main point to bear in mind on all of these wall plays is that variety, surprise, and planning will net you goals. Practice all of the forms of free-kick play—around the wall, through the wall, and over the wall—so that you will be able to execute the appropriate play no matter what the situation and so that the defense will never know what to expect. Read the setup of the defense. Use the free-kick strategy that best utilizes the defense's vulnerabilities. And always set up fast. The faster you work, the more likely you are to catch or force a defender out of position, and thereby to *make* your opportunity rather than to wait for it to come.

Remember that the examples of free-kick

play discussed here are only that—examples. Use your own ideas; think up new methods; work out plays that take advantage of the strengths of your team and of its individual players. If you repeat the same play over and over again just because it worked well a few times, you'll soon find that opposing defenses have tuned in to you and that the play will cease to be effective. Even a tiny variation can be enough to keep the defense guessing. If there is one rule for set plays in soccer, it is this:

Make it new!

THROW-INS

All of your efforts on a throw-in must be directed toward opening players up so that you can retain possession of the ball. Beyond that, a carefully executed throw-in can often start a breakaway play that leaves the defense stunned and flat-footed. (The principles that apply to throw-ins also apply to ordinary free kicks that occur far from either goal and do not involve the creation or the circumventing of a wall.)

Throw-ins, like free kicks, should be taken quickly. Don't give the opposition time to set up its defense! No single concept in soccer could be simpler and more obvious, yet no concept is so widely ignored. Throw-ins should not be taken by an assigned player. In order to move quickly, the player nearest to the ball should take the throw-in. If the whole play is executed with speed, there will probably be at least one unmarked player to receive the throw, and this is the player to whom it should go.

Players can make themselves free to receive the throw by feinting, by calling for the ball as decoys, and by cutting to the inside of their defenders so that there is only space between the thrower and the receiver. The receiver *must* have some free space to work with the ball, since a throw-in is slow and requires more time for effective handling.

Receiving players or potential receivers cannot merely stand around and wait for the throw-in. Everyone must be moving, calling for the ball, running into a space or *creating a space for a teammate* through a run, switching positions with a teammate in order to throw off the defenders, and so on.

Your throw-in need not always go forward. At midfield your fullbacks will often be left unmarked, and a pass back to them can be the most effective move. (Be sure not to twist the ball in mid-throw, however—that's a foul.) You might face a free fullback in an attempt to deceive the defense or to draw a defender back to the fullback, thus opening up a more forward teammate. If the throw-in takes place near your own penalty area, look for your goalie. He can be the safest receiver, and using him as the receiver makes a fast switching of the direction of play easier.

When the throw-in occurs near your opponents' goal, try to work a play whereby you throw to the head of your teammate, who in turn heads the ball up in front of the goal, converting your throw-in into a corner kick. Here, too, your best pass may be backward, since everyone on the field naturally has his attention focused on the goal.

The throw-in itself must be geared to the configuration of your teammates and the defenders. It is not enough to just pick your target and throw. Your throw-in must be placed so that your receiver can use it to best advantage. Depending on the situation, this may mean throwing to his head, so that he can punch the ball over a defender behind him to yet another of your teammates, or it may mean dropping the ball quietly at his feet, so that he can take possession for a dribble or a quick one-touch pass.

One of the most important features of the opposition marking at the throw-in is often overlooked by inexperienced players and teams. The *thrower* is quite frequently left unguarded. This is critical. It means that once the thrower has made his throw he will be an unmarked player when he steps back onto the field. He is available to receive a passback from the player to whom he has thrown the ball. You should always bear this possibility in mind. Even if every receiver is closely marked, one player can come close enough to serve as a "backboard" for the throw, which he in turn one-touches back to the thrower, who has quickly stepped onto the playing field. The rapidity of this move, and the reversal of the ball's direction, may throw the defense off enough to set the original receiver free as well. He then takes a pass, the third in this sequence, from the thrower to whom he has just passed back. This play often works well enough to carry the ball down the touchline before the opposition has quite realized what has happened.

Just as with the free kick around a wall, there are also many ways of creating free space through dramatic tricks. If you are up against a good defensive team, dramatic tricks may be the *only* way you can develop free working space for the throw-in. The idea here is to throw the defensive players off guard, to make them relax for the instant you need to get your play off. One classic English method is to start an argument over who will throw the ball. Two players can tussle with the ball, each claiming that he should be the one to make the throw-in. After the two players argue for a while, the opposing players will relax, expecting a delay in the play. Meanwhile, there are *two* players off the field, and *neither of them is marked.* Upon a prearranged signal one of the "arguers" runs onto the field into an open space and receives the throw from the other "arguer." This is a perfectly legal way of creating an open player, and you should not hesitate to make the opposition think that you are at odds and "untogether" when in fact you are very much together. You can even run this play with three or four players, all standing by the touchline, chatting away. The defense will not know what is going on, will not know what to do, and when the extra players break onto the field like shotgun pellets, surely one of them will manage to get into a free space.

These deceptive tactics can also be used to develop a passback to the thrower. On a throw-in there is no offside, so that the player who breaks into the field for the ball can go completely behind his defender, to be joined there by his thrower and other attackers for a fast break that has *begun behind the defense.*

Plays from the throw-in to create open players are limited only by the number of ideas that you can develop. Someone might throw a coughing fit, or ask the thrower to wait while he ties his shoe—whatever. Remember, there are no time-outs in soccer, and the play goes on whether or not a player asks for one. Also remember that the thrower himself is often

going to be a free player after his throw-in, and that he should be included in your plays.

Practice throw-in plays in nongame situations until they function smoothly and well, with every player knowing his role and the possible variety of his roles. Vary your plays in games, so that the other team will not be able to predict your moves. And never, never, go into a game without a series of set plays that you can use from the throw-in. Your team should always be able to maintain possession from the throw-in, and once your team has developed some tactical skills, it should also be able to generate goal-scoring breakaways, leaving the opposition behind in a muddle of confusion.

CORNER KICKS

Corner kicks probably result in more goals than does any other soccer situation. They are so important that in many leagues corner kicks are used to decide the winner of a tie game (the team that has taken the most corner kicks wins). No team should be without a planned strategy for corner kicks. *Every corner kick represents a potential score.*

The first key to successful corner kick play is to have one or two good kickers. These kickers must be able to loft the ball to the goal with regularity. They should be able to send a ball up to the far post or the near post at will, and they should have the ability to make their kicks swerve inward or outward, depending upon the needs of the play. Unless corner kicks are executed in the air, the defense will pick them up before you have had a chance to use the ball, so be sure that your kickers are consistent and reliable.

Kinds of Corner Kicks

An inswerving kick is harder for your own team to play, but it is also a very difficult ball for the goalie. If the opposing goalie is weak, or slow, try for kicks that swerve in toward the goalmouth. You'll often find, though, that an outswerving kick is more effective in terms of your teammates' follow-through despite the fact that it moves away from the goalmouth. This is because they can run forward into the ball and make a more direct, solid contact. In any event, the swerve is not nearly so important as the fact that the ball should fly across the face of the goal.

The kick can be aimed for several places, each with its own advantages. The actual placement in a game situation will depend on the strengths of your forwards and on the manner in which the defense has set itself up. You can kick to the near post, hoping that one of your players will head the ball inward before the goalie can reach it. A corner kick to the far post will usually rely on a big player who is very good in the aim. You can lay the ball back from the goal, too, at about the eighteen-yard line, for a shot or a second pass by your half. And you should not overlook the possibility of a short kick to one of your players who is out near the corner kicker. This can "entice" defenders out of the goal-mouth and set up a shot, a pass in, or a pass to the corner kicker, who has made a fast run along the goal line toward the goal.

The Placement of Receivers

Forwards should not take up rigid positions to await their chance at a shot. The place to which the ball is going to be centered should be known in advance by all players (you can use a verbal code for this). When the forwards know where the ball will go, they can position themselves deceptively, forcing the defense into false expectations. All of your forwards might line up in a bunch, for example, breaking to prearranged spaces the instant that your corner kicker begins his approach to the ball. The defenders will be confused by this, and they are bound to be a step behind the forwards when the break takes place. Once you have the opposition nervous about your corner kick strategies, you can vary the strategies in infinite ways. Let's say that you want to drop the kick in just past the near post. You can have all of your players line up around the near post, blocking the goalie's ability to see or get to the ball. But he and the rest of his defense may think that you are going to break en masse to the far post, or to the center. In fact, you do *not* break, but provide a mass of strikers exactly where the ball lands. By presenting the defense with a multiple bag of tricks,

you can craftily invent new ones all the time.

Forwards have *one job* on a corner kick—to get to the ball first. Forwards must be utterly aggressive and must blind themselves to the actions of any other players. When the ball comes, it must be one-touched to the goal immediately. There is no time to play with the ball or to bring it under control. If you wait, the defense will block you or take the ball away. You must take your shot instantly, whether it be by head or by foot. Any hesitation can cost the team a goal.

The Movements of the Goalie

Forwards should also remember that the corner kick situation is very rough on the goalie. He has to judge the ball, time his move for it, and keep track of the position of attacking forwards, as well as navigate around the crush of players from both sides who are clogging the goal area. His job is hard, and there's no reason why you, the offense, cannot make it even harder. Stand on the goal line; stand in his way; try to make it difficult for him to judge or get to the ball. You cannot elbow or hit or push the goalie, but there is no rule that prevents you from standing, say, on the goal line between him and the post at which the ball is planned to arrive. After all, you have as much right to play the ball as he does. Don't let him scare you off the ball. You don't have to get out of the way when the keeper goes up for a catch. You can still go up for your header, and you should. Often the goalie will go up slightly out of position because of all the players who are near, and as a result he will miss the ball entirely. He is at a great disadvantage here, and the advantage is yours.

Of course, all of your players must be acutely aware of the movements of the goalie. If he comes out for a ball and fails to field it, every player on your team must know that, and must know that the goal is open. Any player with access to the ball *must shoot* immediately on an open goal. Also watch to see whether the goalie has certain habits, such as coming out of the goal prematurely on high balls, or perhaps staying in too long, and plan the placement of your corner kicks and your strikers accordingly. Whatever your plan, you should always have at least one player at each post, since corner kicks so often result in an unpredictable hurly-burly around the goal and in many near misses that would not be misses at all if there were one last player at the goal corner to put his foot or head on the ball and push it into the nets.

Defensive Marking

Defensive play at corner kicks basically involves "airtight" marking of each member of the opposition and a determined concentration on clearing the ball. The goalie must be especially alert, for he is the defensive fulcrum at all corner kicks. If the ball comes in front of the goal, it is his job to come out and get it. He should have some backup, too, in the form of one defender at each goalpost. When he leaves the goal to go for the ball, these defenders should enter the goal to cover for him—many a corner kick-borne shot has been blocked by a defender who has been covering for an absent goalie. All of the other defenders should stick like glue to the forwards they are marking.

But when the ball comes near you, you must forget about marking and defense. You must forget about everything except that small bit of leather-enclosed space. You must get to the ball. Nothing else matters. Ignore the movements of opposition players. You want the ball above all. Your job is to get it out of the goal area! Forwards on the other team must get a shot at the relatively small goal space. You do not have to set up, nor do you need a special target (though a pass out to one of your upfield players is obviously the best move you can make). You have only one thing on your mind—getting your foot on that ball so that no shot can be taken, and getting your foot on that ball so that you can kick it out of there. You must go to the ball like a lion, a banshee, a lunatic.

If the player you are guarding jumps for a header, go up with him even if he is sure to get to the ball before you do. Your mere presence will make it difficult for him to maneuver and to get off his best shot. You must never let up on the forwards during a corner kick situation. Every moment is dangerous. The real keys to corner kick defense, then, are aggressiveness, concentration, and determination—the same

keys that lead to success in any soccer situation, but all the more important here because of the intense volatility and pressure of the moment.

GOAL KICKS AND GOALKEEPER DISTRIBUTION

Play from a stopped ball at the goal, whether it be a goal kick off the ground or a goalie's distribution through a punt or a throw, can be an occasion for the initiation of a powerful offensive movement, or it can be a time when you merely lose the ball through flaccid and unintelligent play.

The first and foremost premise, frequently ignored by inexperienced players, is that the kick should always go *to* someone. The long boot down the field is rarely effective and is simply not seen in professional play. (There is one situation in which it can be effective—we'll get to that in a moment.)

Goal kicks—awarded to the defensive team when the offensive team kicks the ball past the goal line—should be taken by a fullback if possible. This leaves the goalkeeper guarding the goal in the event of a poor kick or a rapid takeover of possession by the opposing team. The goalie *can* take this kick, but it does seem to be an unnecessary risk to have him do so. The kick should go to the *outside* of the field unless there is a player in the center who is clearly and undeniably unmarked. Again, if the ball is at the outside of the field, there is less danger in the event of a loss of possession. The kick need not be a long one. An accurate pass to a free fullback or half who can begin a move upfield is perfectly adequate. *Never, never,* put the ball across the front of the goal if there is a defender anywhere near.

The more forward players must help out on goal kicks. If they have drifted too far upfield to receive a safe pass, they must come back. If they are marked, they should try to shake their defenders off, perhaps by switching positions with other players. This is critically important for the wings, who are often the final pass receivers on this upfield play.

Keep your goal kicks powerful (to avoid interception) and low (to avoid having an opponent's head pick off the ball as it drifts down gently).

When defenders are not close and are not marking the fullbacks, the goalie and the fullbacks may want to work a play which gives the ball back to the goalie for ordinary distribution. On a goal kick, the ball must leave the penalty area or be touched by an opposing player before the goalie can pick it up with his hands. There are several ways in which the goalie and a fullback—working together—can effect this. The goalie can take the goal kick, passing the ball to the fullback, who is waiting just outside the penalty area (standing to the side of the area, rather than in front of it, is safer and preferable). The goalie follows his pass by running to the fullback. The fullback then taps the ball back to the goalie, who can now pick it up. Alternatively, the fullback can take the goal kick, kicking to the goalie, who is waiting just outside the penalty area. Upon receiving the ball, the goalie dribbles it back into the penalty area (outside that area he cannot touch the ball with his hands) and then picks the ball up.

Obviously, in both of these situations, particularly the latter, great care must be taken to see that there are no opposing forwards who can charge in and intercept the ball. Beware of forwards who may appear uninterested but are waiting for just such a play in order to rush in and execute a steal. Nevertheless, this play does give the ball back to the goalie, who has much greater flexibility in his distribution. It has the disadvantage of taking a great deal of time, time that the opposition can use to tighten up its defense. However, there are periods when the opposition has been applying great pressure and when the best course is precisely to slow down the pace of the game, to break the rhythm of the opposition. (As we have often said, the general rule is to get your plays off fast, before the opposition has a chance to set up, but general rules always have important exceptions.) There are times during a hard-fought match when even halfs at midfield may want to send the ball back to the goalie simply to slow down the game. This is one of the many tools that your team can use to make the course of a match go the way your team wants it to go, and your team should use every tool at its disposal.

Although long balls are no longer a significant part of top-class soccer, there are indeed times when the long goal kick or punt by the goalie can function with the same potency as the touchdown bomb in American football. But the long kick must be set up. If you have a goalie who can punt deep into enemy territory, or a fullback who can make superlong kicks, let him spend the early part of the game making short kicks only. Try to get the opposing fullbacks to feel that there is no danger that a long ball will be lofted over their heads. Have your forwards play toward your own goal when your team is on defense, drawing the opposing fullbacks up with them.

Then, when the fullbacks have been drawn too far forward, and are not anticipating a long ball, the kicker should call out a verbal code to alert his forwards as he boots the ball high over the heads of the defense. The forwards will no doubt be faster than the defenders, and the long kick will function as a through pass which they can pick up and ram in for a score. As a strategic weapon, the long ball is wonderful. Set up properly, it can reward you with goals. But it is a useless play if the defending fullbacks are either expecting it or are in good position to intercept it, and the long ball will never be effective if it is used repetitiously.

THE THEMES OF SET PLAYS

A few *themes* run through all set-piece play, and now is a good time to recall them. Set plays should be taken quickly—don't give the opposition any time at all to set up. They should be based on a planned strategy, and a team should develop several approaches to each kind of situation so as not to become predictable. Each player must know his assignment. Dramatic tactics that throw the other side off are both legal and useful, and your players should learn to become stage players as well as soccer players. The best defense against set plays is alert and tight marking. And for both offense and defense, the style and manner of play of the other side should be under constant scrutiny. Soccer is a game of ideas as well as a game of action, and you can conquer the opposition through the excellence of your ideas—ideas that capitalize on your own strengths and on the opposition's weaknesses.

8
Alignments and Tactics

Soccer is, of course, much more than a game in which eleven players in good condition who have mastered certain skills take the field against an opposing eleven. Because the field is large, and the game swift, each soccer player must be delegated responsibilities. It's a team game, after all, and a team, like any other organization, must assign different roles to each of its members in the hopes of creating a whole that works together smoothly and consistently.

Too, soccer is a game—and this point is often overlooked—of mind as well as body. The strengths and weaknesses of your team and of the opposition must be analyzed, and a plan of action formulated to deal with them. You need a strategy just as a military unit needs a strategy, and you need tactics to make that strategy a reality. Confusing and deceiving the opposition can play an important role in winning matches—the best teams *surprise* their foes as well as outrun and outplay them.

There are many ways to cover the field, move the ball, and stop opposing attacks. In this

chapter we'll explore some of those ways. Our exploration will approach the problem from two angles:

1. Methods of positioning players on the field, which we'll call *alignments*.
2. Methods of teamwork and play that take place *within* a given alignment.

THE HISTORY OF ALIGNMENTS

The task of an alignment is to find the most logical and rational way to cover the field on offense and defense. Perhaps the best way to examine alignments and the forces of the game that call them forth is to spend some time viewing the history of alignments (also called systems) in soccer. As older formations became inefficient through the discovery of their vulnerabilities by astute coaches, new formations had to be invented. A process of perfection has taken place in soccer, whereby the disadvantages of an old alignment were corrected by yet another alignment. The history of alignments reads something like the history of military and business strategy in the West. The trend, as you will see, has always been toward flexibility, streamlining, increased versatility of players, increased teamwork, and, interestingly, a defensive posture.

As you will see, new alignments and systems were created by a thoughtful approach to the game. And the possible ways to set up a soccer team have by no means been exhausted. As you read, think about the reasons why the various changes happened as they did, about how *you* would have responded were you coaching or playing at the time, and about what kinds of alignments you can set up *now* to help your team or to take advantage of your opponents' weaknesses. Soccer thinking, like the game itself, is always in flux, and there is always room for a new idea.

The 2–8 Formation

In the early days soccer was not a team game. It was called the dribbling game, and rightfully so. In this initial incarnation each player dribbled the ball as long as he could, hoping to retain control long enough to take a shot. The idea of a player giving support to a teammate went only as far as his being in the teammate's vicinity to take over a loose ball on the chance that the teammate might lose it on the dribble. No one passed; every player was a star of sorts; and the end of each game must have seen twenty-two very fatigued soccer players.

The English had been playing with one goalie, one fullback, and nine players, as it were, on attack. But in 1872 they met with a Scottish team that employed, of all things, *passing!* Uncharacteristically, the English embraced this new development, which they called combination play, and the modern form of soccer, with teamwork and passing, was adopted rapidly. The Scots showed the English another wrinkle—the use of a second fullback. This too was quickly taken up in England, a development which marked the beginning of a long trend toward defensive soccer. At the beginning of play, then, the English had one goalie, two fullbacks, and eight forwards, a 2–8 alignment.

(Soccer alignments are referred to by numbering the players in the back, middle, and front sections of a team's total configuration. The numbers start from the back, go toward the forwards, and do not include the goalie.)

The 2–3–5 Pyramid

The 2–8 formation went through a series of evolutions which brought into being the notion of midfield play (linkmen and halfbacks) as an initial defensive screen and a way of starting long plays from the backfield. As the value of midfield control became apparent, the 2–8 became the 2–1–7, then the 2–2–6, and finally the classic 2–3–5 formation known as the pyramid, which was for many years the only alignment used in soccer anywhere. The pyramid remained in widespread use in the United States right through the 1960s. It employed two fullbacks, two wing halfs and a center half, and five linkmen (two wings, two insides, one center forward). It is from the 2–3–5 that we have received our current names for players, which are often inappropriate in the new systems in use today.

The appearance of the 2–3–5 on the field is shown in the accompanying diagram. The arrows indicate the approximate range of territory covered by each player.

Bearing in mind the fact that in discussing the pyramid (or any other alignment) we are talking about *general areas* covered by players and about the look of the team as it lines up for a kickoff—*not* strict locations at which each player must stay throughout the game (alignments are more flexible than that)—let's look at the workings of the pyramid. It remained the major system of play until 1925 everywhere in the world, and, depending on the makeup of the competing teams, it may still find effective application today.

The two fullbacks were usually big players. Their responsibility was totally defensive, and they rarely ventured even as far as the midfield line. They functioned something like the dragons which guarded the Golden Fleece. Farther up, the three halfbacks served as a first line of defense, picking up opposing attackers and loose balls at midfield before any damage could

Fig. 19. This is a diagram called the Pyramid. Play on the field is fluid; players rarely move in "lines" across the field.

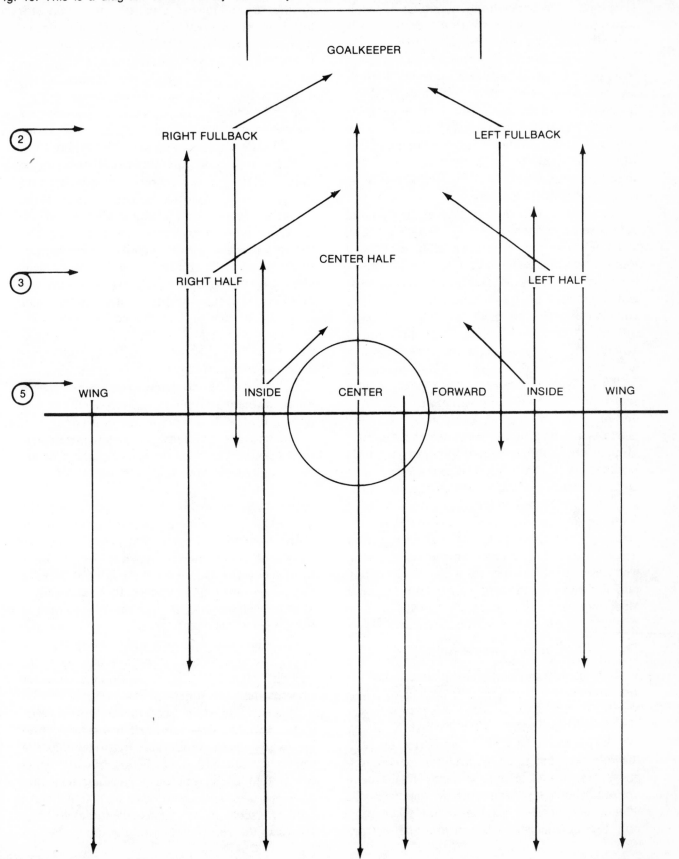

become severe. The halfs followed the offensive play into the opposition's territory as well, which meant that they were almost constantly in motion, covering perhaps two-thirds of the field. The five forwards stayed forward for the most part, awaiting balls sent up by the halfs or the classic long kicks of the fullbacks. The two insides were often required to drop back on defense, but their basic mission was offensive. Wings waited outside for a pass, then headed willy-nilly down the touchline. Center forwards were scrappers, fighters, goal scorers, and often tall for a heading advantage.

The static, rather rigid quality of the pyramid gave rise to the typically English kick-and-run style of play. The Blackburn club introduced long passes successfully in 1883, and for over forty years long passes became the name of the game. Goalies booted the ball as far as they could. Fullbacks boomed their kicks, seeking distance rather than accuracy or the initiation of a play. The long pass out to the wing became a hallmark of offensive play. Up and down the field the ball went, back and forth, constantly subject to turnovers. The game was not really one of ball control as we know it. The subtlety of close interpassing was missing, and the pace of play was uniformly rapid—today the style would look sloppy. But because the ball was moving harder now, and was in the air more, players were forced to develop better skills of trapping and heading. Those skills became increasingly important as soccer evolved toward a more balanced approach on the field. Still, when you are playing a team that is definitely out of condition, the long ball from a pyramid alignment may be just the thing to beat it.

The Change in the Offside Rule

In 1925 a movement to change the critical offside rule gained considerable momentum and finally succeeded in effecting a major change. Up to that time, defenses had learned to use the offside trap with great cunning. Prior to 1925 the rule was that there must be *three* defenders between an attacker and the goal. The moment an opposing player threatened, one fullback would race upfield, leaving the attacker with only two defenders in front of him and *offside*.

Even if the departing fullback's timing was off, or the referee missed the call, there was still another fullback (plus the goalie) on defense. The net result of all this was that fewer and fewer goals were being scored because attackers were being pulled offside so frequently. To answer this problem the offside rule was changed, and this change paved the way for many innovations, whose combined effect was to create the diverse modern styles of play.

The new offside rule required that there be only *two* opponents between the attacker and the goal, as opposed to the earlier three. Now, in order to pull the attacker offside both fullbacks would have to run forward, leaving only the goalie to defend if the referee should happen to miss his call. Under those circumstances, obviously, the offside ploy was pulled far less often. Goal totals for the professional leagues rose immediately.

The 3–4–3, or W–M

That same year, 1925, the Arsenal club made a move to beef up its defense which has led to innumerable variations in the way teams are set up on the field. The club introduced a third fullback. Now that may not seem particularly earthshaking, but the subtle changes that resulted are really quite fascinating.

The center half, previously the midfield playmaker and the mastermind of the team, was moved back to become the third fullback—the center back, or "stopper." This left the midfield weakened, so the two insides were drawn backward to fill the gap. With the two halfs and the two insides at midfield there were now four men patrolling the area, with only three forwards left on the line. This may seem like a boring and utterly defensive system, but it is not. The insides were also attacking players, playing "both ways" completely, performing a kind of cross between their old functions and those of the old halfbacks. The attack became a more layered affair, with the dropped-back insides functioning as playmakers and backward outlets as the center forward and wings (who obviously must cut in frequently) put on a constant thrusting offensive pressure.

The Arsenal 3–4–3, also called the W–M is shown in the accompanying diagram.

Fig. 20. The Arsenal 3–4–3.

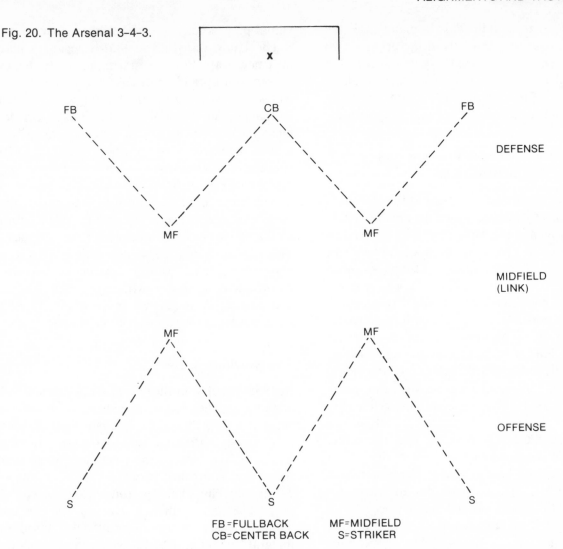

FB=FULLBACK
CB=CENTER BACK

MF=MIDFIELD
S=STRIKER

The changes went beyond a rough diagram of the team in its zone. Most of the players took on new roles in this system, and the entire equilibrium of the team was altered by the addition of another fullback. Greater versatility was required of every player on the field. As you can see, the third fullback was a little change that meant a lot.

Until World War II there were few changes in these two formations. The British used a 3–4–3 almost exclusively, whereas the Eastern Europeans and the South Americans continued to use the old 2–3–5. A successful variation called the metado won the Italians World Cups in 1934 and 1938. The metado was really nothing more than a 2–3–5 alignment with the M half of the 3–4–3 W–M tacked on in front, for attack. The insides were dropped back, confusing opposing defenses and giving the Italians a "second wave"

of offense without sparing a third player for the center back. The metado was a 2–3–2–3, and it is still seen occasionally.

New Roles for Players as Alignments Change

The world changed after World War II, and so did soccer. The success of the 3–4–3 had caused coaches everywhere to realize that there were other possibilities for positioning players. A new era of experimentation began to take hold as it became apparent that a system of play was just as important as skills and conditioning. There are no rules about alignments. You can set up players and assign them responsibilities in any way that you choose. What matters is that your system work.

By 1954 virtually every world class team was

using at least three fullbacks. In many cases the third back was dropped behind the original two fullbacks, becoming what we now call the sweeper. The sweeper, or libero, was basically a free player, the last player back, who could move anywhere to cut off a threatening attack.

The Withdrawn Center Forward and the Hungarian Attacking W

The new emphasis on defense and the introduction of the center back posed an obvious problem for a team's offensive unit. The center forward, who had previously been a relatively free player between the original two fullbacks, open and ready to score when passed to, was stymied. The center back marked him player-to-player at all times, and the center forward was nearly eliminated from his formerly potent offensive role. The Hungarian teams of the early fifties, the "Magic Magyars," introduced the *withdrawn center forward* to cope with this problem. They used a five-player offensive line, but the center forward dropped back behind his insides and wings. This meant that the center back, who was assigned to mark the center forward, had no one to guard. The center back could not risk being drawn out to where the center forward was playing, yet he became an extra player if he remained back with the other fullbacks.

The center forward, in turn, was freed up to become the playmaker, taking on the former role of the attacking center halfback. The center forward was no longer the main goal scorer, but he was left free to distribute passes, to set up plays, to serve as a backward passing outlet and a way station for balls being switched across field, and to move in for a shot when the middle was open. The wings were pulled back slightly (not so much as the center forward), so that the new Hungarian offense came to be called, from its appearance, the attacking W. The formation was fluid, since the withdrawn center forward could also be pressed into defensive midfield service when his team was under pressure. Sometimes the formation was a 3–2–5, other times a 3–3–4, and while the formation was still fresh and still surprising opposition defenses, it produced many victories over teams whose indi-

vidual players may often have been stronger.

The Hungarian fullbacks also began to play in a new way. For the first time, the fullbacks moved well upfield on offense, working with the wings and covering midfield along with the two halfbacks who remained in the 3–2–5. On defense they had to run back quickly. This newly mobile defensive play, in which the traditional concept of a strict division between offense and defense began to break down, had a powerful impact on soccer and continues to dominate the ideas of soccer thinkers. Fullbacks play as both attacking wing halves and defensive stoppers. This obviously requires a new kind of player, a player who is not simply destructive but also constructive, a player with good ball control and passing skills as well as the ability to stop an opposing forward dead in his tracks.

The Brazilian 4–2–4

In 1958 Brazil won the World Cup with a 4–2–4 alignment. The 4–2–4 had been seen briefly before, in England, but it had never before been a distinctly *offensive* configuration. In the hands, or the feet, of the Brazilians, with their flashy and controlled forward teamwork, the 4-2-4 became an exciting, total team system of play. The extra fullback did not weaken the team's offense, for the wing fullbacks played an integral role on attack. Yet, when the opposition players came deep into Brazil's territory, they found four players back plus the midfielders waiting for them.

On attack, the fullbacks became wing halves or, frequently, extra wings playing just behind the wing forwards. This meant that, if trapped, the wings could go *back* with the ball—an innovation that permitted swift switching of direction (since the fullbacks could send the ball across field) and effective, reckless penetration of opposing defenses. The wing fullbacks, as *fullbacks,* were almost never closely marked by the opposition defense. Who could be spared to go out and guard them? The 4–2–4, then, looking deceptively like a defensive alignment, actually became a 2–4–4 on offense. A 2–4–4 would have simply been too weak defensively if it had been a constant alignment, but it was not. The alignment was created only by an offensive drive. When the ball turned over, it was up to the fullbacks to hustle back toward their own goal, leaving the midfield chores to midfielders. The midfield was strengthened on defense by the withdrawal of at least one winger, so that the defensive alignment was in fact a 4–3–3. Thus the 4–2–4 was perhaps only a shorthand for a fluid, flexible system that became a 2–4–4 or a 4–3–3, or even a 4–4–2, as the occasion demanded. Opposing teams were confused and often outmanned as the Brazilians flooded the field with up to eight players on offense and seven or eight on defense. In effect, the Brazilians created a situation in which they were able to *outnumber* the opposition, as if Garrincha, Pele, and company were not already enough.

The Italian 5–3–2, 4–3–3

During this modern period, the Italians became the masters of the decidedly defensive game. Their alignment, the Catenaccio, was perhaps the most conservative that has ever been seen in soccer. It's possible that Italy's defeat in the war coupled with the dreadful state of the Italian economy had led even Italian *soccer players* to choose the safest, most protected path possible. Whatever the reason, Italian teams became known for their stubborn penalty-area barricades. The Italian teams worked from a 4–3–3 and even a 5–3–2, turning the old pyramid upside down in their efforts to prevent the wound of an opposing goal. A line of three fullbacks was supplemented by a fourth, a libero or sweeper, playing behind the other fullbacks. On occasion, the Italians would use *five* fullbacks, clearly leaving few players to do their scoring. If a team can break out of this kind of rock-hard defense for a long drive downfield, the system works fine. If not, the team defeats itself, for loading up so many players in the backfield means that the opposition will have control of the ball in the midfield—and from the midfield be able to mount attack after attack on the wary Catenaccio.

Other developments followed logically from the new emphasis on both defense and the increased versatility of defensive players that was sweeping the soccer world. It may seem paradoxical that both offensive and defensive play were being strengthened at the same time. One would think that a stronger offense would mean a weaker defense, but in fact the soccer world was witnessing an increase in total efficiency. More players were being asked to do more things. When it became clear that they could, the *overall* level of soccer rose correspondingly.

In a moment we shall come to the inevitable conclusion that the evolution of soccer had to reach. But first let's look at some of the additional improvements or experiments that were seen on major teams.

The Upcenter Fullback

A new position was added, that of the defensive screen or upcenter fullback. This player was the sweeper, whom we have already seen, moved up to play *in front of* the line of fullbacks. Instead of functioning as a last stopper, as did the sweeper, the defensive screen broke up the play *before* the opposition was able to mount penetrating momentum. The opposing center forward was never free now—even if he hung back, the screen player was able to follow and mark him closely.

The role of the wing was markedly deemphasized. The new four-, three-, or even two-player line simply did not include enough players to spread out that far. This is not to say that the touchline run disappeared from view. The sides were often empty now, leaving free space for a fast striker to take the ball outside or for a midfielder or a fullback to charge down the touchline in an unpredictable "second wave" of offense.

There were only two or three forwards, and these came to be called strikers, for the old names no longer seemed to apply. Instead of trying to move the ball straight down the field and to work in channels in front of their assigned positions, strikers learned to work the ball sideways (the space had become available) and to "flood" an area as a threesome. The idea of support for a teammate with the ball, and strategic running off the ball, became more important than ever.

New room on the field was created for the

expressive player—the inside who could become a wing or a half as the situation demanded; the fullback who could exploit the newly opened-up touchline space with an offensive charge; the libero sweeper who might find himself moving up the center of the field with an intercepted ball at his feet; the player who learned to cover for a teammate who had seized the moment, whether on offense or on defense.

Clearly these developments pointed in only one direction for the future of soccer—greater fluidity and flexibility, more organic movement, and *less* reliance on alignments and the mechanical oversimplification that they imply.

The Whirl, or "Total Football"

The powerful German and Dutch teams of the sixties and seventies introduced a system of play that came to be known as the Whirl—it is also known as *total football*—in which every player was expected to be able to run all the time and to take up whatever position the lay of the play required. In *The Simplest Game* (Boston: Little, Brown, 1976), Paul Gardner cites the journalist Willy Meisl as follows:

> In my opinion the future belongs to *The Whirl*. It must rotate on *individuality* rooted in *all-round capacity*. . . . a fullback seeing an opening up front must seize his chance without hesitation. A wing half or winger will fall back, if necessary, and being an all-rounder, will not feel uncomfortable or out of place. The consciousness that he is also a forward will give the back's thrust weight and impetus. The knowledge that whoever has taken over from him (behind his back) will make a good job of it should the occasion arise, will enable him to carry on with his action (raid) without undue hurry or nervousness. He must and will be sure that he has left no exposed flank behind himself.

THE FLEXIBILITY OF ALIGNMENTS

The Whirl, then, or total football, is at the center of the modern game. Alignments are now intellectual formulations that give us a good indication of how the field needs to be covered both on offense and on defense, but they do not tell us that each player *must* stay in his "position" at all times, no matter what is happening on the field. On the contrary, players must now possess all the skills necessary to play anywhere, and they must be prepared to move when the opportunity presents itself. Likewise, each player must now maintain an acute awareness of the locations of all the other players and be ready to fill in when a teammate moves to take advantage of an opportunity or to plug up a hole. Whether on defense or on offense, players must keep in mind not only their own responsibilities but also how they can contribute to the play of the team as a whole.

Soccer, which is a battle of sorts, has changed in much the same way that military battles have changed. Once, two regiments lined up across a field from each other, knelt, and fired willy-nilly. Now attacks and defensive systems are computer-controlled, lightning swift, and constantly subject to tactical adjustments, and they utilize special units that go into action when the time is right. Your team must play the same way. If the ball is to be carried up the right touchline, the fullback, the right striker, and the right midfielder must form a temporary "special unit" to accomplish the mission. When the ball is switched across the field, some members of the special unit may go with it, and others drop off as new teammates take their places. The game has a much more intuitive quality now— the move that *feels* right probably *is* right.

The initial lineup, or alignment, should be balanced, providing good coverage for the entire field. From there, depending on the play, the initial lineup can become a 2–3–5, a 3–3–3–4, a 3–4–3, a 4–4–2, a 4–2–4, a 3–1–2–4, or any other permutation or combination that you can think of. What's important is that there be at least three players forward when the team is on offense, and at least four players back when the team is on defense. It has become clear over the years that these are really minimum figures for effective play.

Any variation is possible. If your team is clearly outclassed, you will want to load up the backfield, Catenaccio-style, and work on developing fast breaks for your scoring opportunities. Against a slower team, on the other hand, you can afford to focus more on offense, for your players will be intercepting the opposition *if* they have learned to cover for each other and to anticipate the potential tactics of the other side.

Your fullbacks may wind up scoring, and your wings may wind up preventing goals. That's fine, as long as all players understand that they cannot remain static. The alignment is no longer the main thing. The crucial features of a team now are the awareness of players, their versatility, and their ability to go anywhere on the field for a full ninety minutes.

TACTICAL INTERRELATIONSHIPS

Whatever basic format you use, however, there are considerations involving tactical and player interrelationships without which you cannot succeed. Alignments are macro-soccer, the big picture. Within the big picture, however, is where everything happens. It is in micro-soccer—the details of play, particularly the strategic details, the small moments, the individual frames that make up the larger motion picture—that you will find the difference between winning and losing teams.

Switching the Direction of Play

Any team that wants to win must learn to utilize smooth teamwork in switching the direction of play. The natural tendency of both the offensive and the defensive side is to bunch in the area near the ball. This is especially true when the ball gets "stuck" in a certain place (a corner, for example) or when one or two players stand out from the rest of the team. When you are on attack, and the defense drifts over toward the ball until it is out of balance, your players should be able to switch the ball to another part of the field instantly. To do this, all players must maintain the awareness that we spoke of earlier. They have got to know where their teammates are, and when a teammate is free. The ball should then be sent quickly to the free teammate, opening up a potentially explosive penetration. The element of surprise, confusion, and change of pace in sharpening your attack can never be overestimated.

You needn't wait for the other side to bunch up near the ball. There's no reason why your team can't employ a conscious tactic of slowing the ball down, perhaps even pretending to be trapped, to *draw* the opposition near the ball. Another way to create good switching opportunities is to play the ball consistently to only one side of the field. Then, when the opposition players have been lulled into thinking that they know what to expect, you can suddenly switch the area of play to another space. You may even want to try holding your players out of this space during the deception phase. Then, when you're ready to switch the play, your player enters the free zone upon a prearranged signal. Remember, you're trying to trick the opposition—any method that you can think of is fine as long as it works.

Of course, you can't always create a switching opportunity. Often you'll be forced into a situation in which you *have* to send the ball far from its present area. This ability is critical, and your team should work on it in practice until the skill becomes second nature and an integral part of your team's basic playing rhythm.

Often, inexperienced players believe that the ball should be pushed forward, and only forward, in every situation. But if you watch professional teams for only a few minutes you'll see that this is far from the truth. Frequently the best play is backward. When the passage of a ball across the field is blocked by defenders, the player *behind* you may well have a better angle—one good enough to send the ball over to your "switchee," your free player. Your awareness must extend behind you as well as in front and to the sides. And the player behind the ball carrier should always call out "Help behind!" or something similar so that the carrier is well aware of the available outlets.

On the other hand, beware of the switched play or the backward play when you are deep in your own territory. Here, misplaying the ball may set up an opportunity for an opposition goal. Deep in your own area, the switched or backward play is a risky play rather than a clever one. And *never, never, never,* unless you are a world class fullback, switch the ball across field in front of your own goal. This is probably the most dangerous play in soccer.

Communication

Whether the ball is being switched across field, interpassed in one area, sent long, or carried by a dribbler, the crucial ingredient that makes a team jell is *communication*. Communication is perhaps the best soccer strategy of all. For it's not always easy to keep your head in soccer. The tension of being directly involved in a play may confuse you. You may forget where your teammates are, or their positions may have changed rapidly. You need to *hear* them tell you where they are; you need to hear them tell you where your best play is. Every member of the team should learn to *talk*. Learn to call for the ball when you are open, or to call out where the carrier should pass the ball when you are not. Verbal codes are good too. You can confuse your opposition if you develop a code that lets everyone on your team know that a player is *not* free, although he calls for the ball as if he were.

But don't let this idea backfire, and through it try to realize one of the keys to good communication. Calling out will help the team immeasurably—it will make the team a well-oiled machine rather than a rusty one; it will be the glue that holds the parts together—*but only when the right players are calling out the right things*. Nothing will foul a team up more than a player who calls for the ball when he is not free or when he is not in the best position to move the ball. Team members must learn to *keep quiet,* too. Keep quiet when you are not useful. Don't call for the ball just because you want it—this is the most common mistake of novices. Only call for the ball when you are the player who is in the best position to move the ball. Or call to tell one of your teammates to fill a space or to mark an opponent he doesn't see. Or call to the ball handler if you see the right play and he doesn't. But don't call out just to say hello. Don't make your teammates rely on ESP. Call out. But call out as a thoughtful tactician, not as a player who wants to be in the middle of the action as often as possible.

THE ELEMENTS OF A WINNING SOCCER TEAM

Many different countries have fielded many different great soccer teams, teams whose style of play and tactics have varied enormously. But there are constant features that reappear in all top teams. If your team works hard at incorporating each element into its play, you can be sure that you will be playing, if not winning soccer, *at least* the best possible soccer with the players available. And you can count on winning far more games than you would if you merely sent out eleven players to boot the ball around in disorganized and sloppy confusion.

Every great soccer team must:

1. *Be in top condition.* Soccer is a running game. That should never be forgotten.

2. *Set up a balanced alignment of players on the field and make sure that players know when to leave their "positions," when not to, and when to cover for a teammate who has moved.*

3. *Support the ball handler by moving into open spaces to become outlets for a pass.*

4. *Communicate—the appropriate message at the appropriate time.*

5. *Master the fundamentals of soccer before taking the field.* This applies to both individual skills and team ball control. If the team members cannot trap and pass and dribble and kick, you haven't really *got* a soccer team! The basic mode of play in soccer is passing. The team must practice its passing—with defenders trying to interfere—for hours and hours and hours. So many situations can occur in a game that you can never practice them all, but you can practice the *kinds* of situations that always occur. Wall passes, triangular interpassing, squaring, through passes, cross-field passes, back passes, long passes, high passes, chips, corner kick passes, throw-in plays, and so on.

The same goes for the basic modes of defense.

6. *Be able to switch the direction of play.* The team whose play is predictable is the team that will quickly become stymied by a confident opposition defense.

7. *Be able to change quickly from offense to defense, and be able to get an attack going **fast** once possession of the ball is recovered.*

8. *Establish target players whom the defense can play the ball up to.* Some players must always stay forward, or a team will have great difficulty in moving the ball out of its own half of the field. When the defense gains possession, it should know where the target players are, so that it can pass the ball up to them virtually automatically.

9. *Thoroughly master set plays.* There is no excuse for blowing a free-kick play, either on offense or on defense. The corner kicks, those most goal-productive of opportunities, should be worked on at every single practice.

10. *Learn to control the pace of the game.* Do this, and you will have 25 percent of the battle won. If the opposition players are controlling the ball with slow and careful precision, you must recognize this and begin to rush them, force them to play the ball faster and to make mistakes in passing or trapping. By the same token, you must learn to slow down your own play when it gets sloppy. There's no sense in pressing harder and harder when things aren't going well. Slow down—slow down and take stock. Slow down and focus on ball control and ball possession. Work to create space for yourselves on the field.

11. *Learn to avoid "dumb" mistakes, particularly on defense near your own goal.* So many goals are "garbage goals" that should never have been conceded. Defenders must always put pressure on the player with the ball, must always support any of their number who go out of position to stop a play, must always pick up a player who is dangerously close to the goal (whether or not he has the ball, whether or not he is now near the ball), must always avoid "playing with the ball"—that is, must always pass it upfield crisply and quickly—when it is in their own territory.

12. *Make all its passes to a teammate.* That sounds like the most elementary of catechisms. If it were followed invariably, there would be no need to stress the point. Never just kick the ball away. After all, the name of the game is control.

13. *Develop a winning attitude.* Again, the principle seems elementary. But so many teams, even world class teams, ignore it. The 1974 Brazilian team is a prime example. Afraid that its scoring punch was gone, since it no longer had Pele, the team huddled back in its own territory, hoping to stop goals, forgetting about scoring them. And the team didn't score. And it lost the World Cup. The Brazilian players were well able to score on any team in the world. But they didn't believe it. So, of course, they didn't score.

If your forwards seem to take too much time before a shot, somehow always being blocked by an opposing fullback or never quite beating the goalie, this may well be a failure of attitude rather than a failure of skill. A team must be willing to draw blood, to give all it's got, to keep its cool at all times, to tackle opposing dribblers fearlessly.

TIPS FROM THE STARS: THE GREAT TEAM

The great team must be good in every department, but it does not necessarily have to excel everywhere—it must be solid. There must be an all-around effort, everyone must do their best and help each other. The players must make up for whoever is having a bad day—identify the off players and compensate for them. You're never going to get all eleven players at their tops. The great team is great at making the *fast* change from defense to offense, never giving the other side a chance to recover. Above all, the great team has learned *how to get the ball in the net!!!*

Giorgio Chinaglia

The great team has good players, a good coach, a desire to go on and win, often a winning tradition, and, above all, teammates who get along. Team unity is a very big part of the game.

Alan Mayer and Arnold Mausser

The great team must have material—the players—and they must be players who can *play offense and defense at the same time.* Then, the players must play together as a team—you can't have too many individual players. You need a good coach too, and he must make the right calls and substitutions.

Steve Ralbovsky

What makes for a great team?

1. *Friendship and respect*—when the teammates are friends and respect each

other (and that takes time to develop), then they work with and *for* each other.

2. *Dedication to the success of the team*—if all the players are just interested in their own glory, the team will never be a real winner.

3. *Support*—working together and *for* each other is the key.

Bobby Smith

1. All the players have to have a general understanding of each other, what each other's strengths and weaknesses are, and be able to use them.

2. The team has to be willing to sacrifice themselves for each other, interchanging positions, creating openings, taking on different roles, yet never losing sight of where you are and what your responsibilities are.

3. The team must be able to go from defense to offense quickly and constructively. Eleven players on offense and eleven players on defense.

4. A team needs a keen sense of possession and must be unwilling to give the ball up easily.

5. Everyone must work together to create scoring chances.

Al Trost

On a great team the players must know each other and communicate well. They have to know what to expect from each other—you need to know what your man will do in a certain situation. And a great team needs a great coach to point out tactics that are going to help you work together as a team. You need a game plan that attacks the other team's weaknesses. Every great team has a coach that the team *wants* to play for. When the coach is a *friend*, you want to win for him.

What makes a great team? Eleven players who go both ways. You have to have eleven offensive players, and the same eleven as defensive players, for a full ninety minutes. That's the only answer.

Greg Villa

If a team as great as Brazil could be beaten by attitude, you should scrutinize your own most carefully.

14. *Outhustle the opposition.* If there is a loose ball, your players must get to it first. If there were records kept to tell us which teams picked up the most loose balls in World Cup play, the teams on top would surely also be the teams that won the most games.

15. *Do what was first described at the very beginning of this book—form and reform to* **carve out space on the field.** Remember, you are not just playing with a ball and twenty-two men. You are also playing with space.

9
Scoring...
An Interview
with Derek Smethurst

Derek Smethurst began his career at age sixteen in South Africa, scoring thirty-eight goals in two seasons with the Durbin City club. From there he moved to the English professional leagues, playing a total of seven and one-half years with Chelsea and Milwall. Then, in 1975, coach Eddie Firmani picked up Derek as a free agent to play for the Tampa Bay Rowdies (where he is still the star striker). In 1975 Derek was second in scoring and second in total points in the NASL. In 1976 he was top scorer and second in points, and in 1977, just to assure himself and everyone else that his prowess was no flash in the pan, he was again second in scoring and second in overall points. Of course, Derek is a regular on the NASL All-Star teams. If anyone knows what you must know about scoring goals, it is Derek Smethurst.

When I'm trying to score, all I'm concentrating on is beating one man, the last defensive player. I don't try to go around every man back there, just to beat the last man. I'm a touch player—when the ball comes to me, I like to touch it off right away, and then to pick up the ball in an *open space* when it comes back to me. Around the goal there is not too much open space, so you have to work extra hard to find and get into whatever open space is available. You've got to start out by thinking that you're better than the other man, that you can go around him and get behind him. Watch him carefully, and *always try to put yourself where he doesn't think you're going to be.*

When you're in front of the goal, your big key to success is remaining *cool*. Most young players don't realize how much time you have in front of the goal. You have more time than you realize, because defenders mostly tend to go into a kind of shock when a striker gains possession in front of the goal—defenders *hesitate* when you get control in front of the goal. For a moment, in horror, they're saying "Oh, no!" before they realize that they have to do something about the situation. Then, because they have defensive assignments, they get confused about who is supposed to go after the man with the ball. This gives you extra time, time to keep

125

Derek Smethurst in action.

Courtesy of Tampa Bay Rowdies.
Photo by Don Lightfoot.

Courtesy of Tampa Bay Rowdies.
Photo by Ed Neubaum.

cool and place your shot. You'll often have a second or two, and that's a lot of time in the goal area—time enough to be sure that you don't strike the ball badly.

Young players should take a little more time. The shot should be *directed,* and bent around to the blind side where the goalie can't see it. It is futile to try and just hammer the ball through—good placement is much more important for your shots. Try to put the ball right into the corner, and keep it low. Poke the ball in from anywhere, change pace on it, always try to confuse the goalie. *Shots should be unexpected.*

So in general, *learn to take your time, but be sure to take your shot.*

When I am near the goal, my golden rule as a striker is: *Don't give the ball away.* Don't try to dribble on someone when you're in the middle of the field—lay the ball off to a teammate, and go to an open space where you can take a pass, go to a place where you can be dangerous. And near the goal, what point is there in trying to dribble the ball around three men? Most players can't do it, and they only wind up giving the ball away. To what purpose? None. As a striker, you've got to lay it off and move—*the good shots come when you're fed, not when you carry it in.*

Ninety-five percent of all goals are scored within six feet of the goal. Don't give the ball away, and don't let it be taken away. Pass off, keep control, fake and feint, experiment, try whatever you can think of—follow my second golden rule, *which is never to be predictable.* The goalie and the defenders must always be kept guessing. If they know what you will do, you won't be able to do it. You must always be creating new and surprising moves.

Even when the ball is away from you, there is much that a striker can and should be doing. If there is great pressure on the defense, the striker can back up slightly and take a midfield position. But remember that there must be at least one man, and preferably two, up front to take the pressure off, to serve as a passing outlet so that the defense will be able to clear the ball upfield. Though you can go back, in general the striker serves a better purpose by maintaining an offensively oriented position.

When you are waiting for the play to come your way you should *never* be standing still. I try to get myself in good position—get into the open space—before the play gets close to me. I make my move as *inconspicuous* as possible—I actually try to *hide* what I am doing when I move around. This means I don't call for the ball too much because this telegraphs the play. If my man is on balance, in control of the ball, and has a clear path to me, only then will I scream for the ball, only when I know he can get off the pass immediately.

When a defender is guarding me and the play is off on another side of the field, I don't try to run away from the defender—that's simply a waste of energy. Instead, I take the defender for a little *walk.* If he doesn't come along with me, then I'm left free, and that's fine. If he does, I'm drawing him out of position and opening up extra space in front of the goal. Either way you can't lose. Unless you want to make the defender stand still for some reason, never stand still yourself. Take him for a little walk down to the goal, take him for a walk out to the touchline, walk him anywhere you please (always keeping an eye out on the play and trying to get yourself most strategically positioned).

The best place to be with a defender—and I always try to maneuver myself there—is one or two yards *behind* him (keeping offside problems in mind). You must remember that the defender can only react *to* you, not *before* you, so that when you make your move you are going to get a three-yard jump on him. This is even more true when you "blind-side" him, when you get yourself positioned *behind* him. If he tries to come back around and get behind you (this is where any good defender should be), then you can just walk around behind him again. Go in circles behind him all the way to the goal line if you have to, but get behind that man. Positioning yourself behind the man is good for at least three yards on him, maybe more, and that's all you'll ever need to make your moves. Keep the defender thinking all the time. You've got to keep yourself moving all the time. Most of a striker's psychological and mental and even physical energy are burned up during a game trying to *outpsych* the defender.

Mental energy is the key. Don't rely on futile and silly running as a striker. Make space and wait—don't give the ball away. Rely on your mind, on guile, not on sheer physical effort. Keep the ball moving more than the body, and always, always, keep making space.

Interpassing is crucial to a striker. The heavy dribbler is a liability, but the great short passer is a fantastic asset. The *great knack for a striker is to be able to play a one-two wall pass.* This skill is absolutely essential—every striker must have it. It's the highest skill for scoring goals. When you take a pass you *always* look for a passback—a way to touch the ball off—first. No man can run as fast as a ball can be passed, and defenders have no time to react to a quick, perfectly executed wall pass play near the goal. If the pass is good, you've beaten a whole wall of defenders. You can even beat ten men if you have to with a wall pass. You can never beat as many defenders with a dribble as you can with a wall pass. Give-and-go, give-and-go—if the ball bounces right, you're all alone for a shot. Great players like Pele even use the opponent's legs for a wall—you don't necessarily need a teammate to get the fast-paced effect of a wall pass.

Going past the goalie and defenders? Every time a shot gets taken on goal, I'm going to follow it in. I'll always be near the goalie because it gives me a *free shot* on goal if he fails to control it. It's always nice to let the goalie know you're there—you've got to make him nervous, try to undercut his confidence. I'll try anything, anything at all—chip shots, bent shots, anything that is a surprise. I often aim a volley shot right at the goalie. Volleys are so hard to control that they *rarely* go where you want—using a kind of inverse logic, if you aim a volley at the goalie, it will probably go somewhere that he isn't. On the shot you always have to *take chances coolly*—don't snatch the ball and get nervous. *Good shots are more important than actual goals,* for if you take good shots the goals will come. When you volley you need absolute concentration, not power, really. If the ball is coming at you at forty miles an hour it will leave your foot at forty miles an hour too. The more shots you take, the more goals you'll score. Never be afraid to take your shot (but you can't shoot from thirty yards out all the time either).

Get in close (most of my own goals are scored from within ten yards). You must always *be there,* you must always be in a place from which you can score. So many goals come from goalies' or defenders' mistakes—more than half my goals come off defensive mistakes. Some people call them garbage goals, but I call them golden goals. They're the most frequent kind. Kids should learn to work on scrapping and hustling near the goalmouth. *Always work on the assumption that the defender will miss the ball—* always get in position to take advantage of a possible defensive mistake. Figure out where the ball will go if there is a mistake, and *go there.* I got two goals last year from just that kind of play. *Anticipate, don't wait!*

The most dangerous play in soccer, and the best scoring play, is when the winger brings the ball down to the end line and then passes it, not exactly across, but *back* and across to the striker who is running directly into the ball. The striker then has both power and maneuverability, while the defenders are all running backward, looking to the corner, and lacking in mobility. If you want to develop one scoring play, it should be this one. I'll give you a twist on it in a minute.

Corner kicks? The best place to be on a corner kick is at the *near post* (the post closest to the corner where the kick is coming from). I stand on the goal line, and I move two yards off the line, getting myself into position to be first man to touch the ball. The corner kick should be low and powerful and right at me. Then I flick it back into the goal. The goalie hasn't got a chance on this play. As an alternative, I'll go out to the eighteen-yard line opposite the far post and come running diagonally across the goal area to the near post. This is an exceedingly dangerous play on a hard hit near post cross, my most consistent scoring play and my favorite "secret" for scoring. The cross should be no higher than head high. The typical chip ball on the cross is *no good*—it's too hard to score from. The hard ball is best, not the high ball. The ball must have pace on it to be good for scoring. Always be asking yourself, "Where might the ball land?" Take the chance and go there. Don't wait to see what happens—by then it will be too late.

Scoring happens when the ball is taken down the line and behind the fullback and then passed back to the striker, who is running in hard. I hate to repeat myself, but this play causes so much trouble and results in so many scores that I want to be sure all young players and all coaches realize how effective it can be.

Always keep changing the ball. Change the pace, change the kind of kicks and passes, change the direction. Again, never be predictable. Scoring is an art in which you constantly have to create new patterns that open up space for you to work in.

When can you beat the goalie? You should always try to fake him out, surprise him, put it where he thinks it won't go. But the real time you can beat the goalie is when he comes out on you. When he's coming out at top speed he has virtually no maneuverability—he can't stop quickly, he can't move from side to side. The minute a goalie comes near me when he's running, I shoot. The element of surprise is the key, and I'll try anything. If he comes diving at my feet, I'll chip it up over his body, but in almost every other case I try to keep my shots low. Low shots are much harder for the goalie to get. He can't react fast enough: he has to both go for the ball *and* drop down—that takes too long. Also you can often get a favorable bounce on a ground ball. To keep the ball low, keep your head down, your eye on the ball, and your toe pointed down. You've got to be like a ballet dancer, always pointing your toe down. Contact the ball up on your instep, where it's hard and powerful, *not* on the top of your toes, and *follow through*. If you lean back you'll pop it up. Follow-through gives you other parts of your body to hit the ball with in case you miss. I've knocked in goals with my shins, my knees, and even my backside—*everything's* a weapon when you're trying to score.

But so far we've been talking about only *half* a striker. To be whole a striker must have great aerial power. You're only half a striker unless you're good in the air—it's *so* important to be good in the air.

Practice every day to get good in the air. Take

crosses; jump up as high as you can; use your hips and back as well as your neck. Head toward the far post *always*—that way, if you miss it, the ball can still go in the near post. Timing is so important too: if you get up a fraction of a second before your opponent you've beaten him—the *force* of your body pushes him down. Try to hang up there—learn how to go up and hang. Always watch the other player to see when he's going up—try to be on his blind side so he can't see you—and then go up an instant before he does. This will improve your air play immensely, just this simple emphasis on getting up in the air a fraction of a second before your defender. You've got to be *brave* in the air: There's no other way to say it—courage is really needed. But remember, anybody that's really good in the air is going to score goals.

You can never stop learning—it's a game of continuous creation. The main thing American kids have to learn is not to be afraid to shoot on goal. I see so many kids with great moves getting themselves into scoring position, but then they blow it because they freeze up—they're afraid to shoot.

My top secret is to move from the *blind side* of my defender (where he can't see me well) from the far post to the near post right across the whole line of defense. I *won't stop running,* even if the ball isn't coming to me, because the run will still create space by drawing off a defender or two. Take daylight when you see it—that's what American players have to learn, that and to take shots when you've got them. Every great striker has his own strong points, and he *plays to them*. Work on your weaknesses during practice, but play to your strengths during the game. Play to your assets—anything else is futile and silly. George Best has the fakes and feints; Steve David has great speed over three yards; Chinaglia gets up high in the air and knows how to get into open space—every great scorer is different. There's no one rule: you just have to think all the time, scheme all the time, and hustle all the time, while you play to your assets.

And improvisation is the greatest asset of all.

10 Training

Ninety minutes is a long time to run. The team that is in the best condition has a powerful advantage, and the player who tires least will stand out when all the other players on the field have their tongues hanging out. Too, soccer is fundamentally a game of ball control and movement. In order to be successful in matches you must break down the individual and team components of ball control and practice them in isolation. Conditioning and skills—these really separate the players from the dabblers.

CONDITIONING

You need to develop:

1. *Endurance*—the ability to run for a full game without tiring.
2. *Speed off the mark*—the ability to cover short distances quickly from a standing start or a turn.
3. *Overall running speed.*

There is truth to the maxim "Soccer is for speedsters." But the most important movement ability is speed off the mark, not necessarily the capacity to run a hundred yards in ten seconds.

Endurance

Building up your endurance is conceptually simple. What's hard is doing it. You have to run and run and run. The more you run, the more endurance you will have. That's the cold reality.

Run to the field where you play. Take a few laps when you get there. When you have to chase a ball, run to get it. After practice or a game, run some more. Take extra laps. Then run home.

Since in game situations you will have to run in different ways, your workouts should reflect this. You should spend some time at an even jog, some time in fast sprints, some time running backward, and some time running sideways.

There is only one way to expand your endurance, no matter what techniques you use for the actual running. You must progressively increase the quantity of your workouts. In this case, quantity becomes quality. If you start out running three laps, you should shortly build up to four, then five, then six, and so on. Only by increasing the amount of running that you do will you be able to assure yourself of being able to play for ninety minutes, as strong at the end of the match as at the beginning. So a daily mile or so simply isn't enough. You have to learn to go longer, and farther, until you reach the point at which you don't tire significantly in a game.

TIPS FROM THE STARS: CONDITIONING

The one ingredient in soccer that hasn't changed from the times when you would run from one village to the other is *stamina*. And it is the main ingredient in soccer—more so than size or speed. In soccer you have to prepare yourself for physical exhaustion. I probably lose eleven or twelve pounds a game and run seven or eight miles. I've never played a sport that demands a player to be in better physical condition.

Kyle Rote, Jr., Beyond the Goal

One way to build up your endurance is to use ankle weights or heavy clothing. If you practice running with a great deal more weight than you would ordinarily carry, you will build your muscles a great deal faster. When you remove the weights you will feel light as air when running, and your newly strengthened legs will carry you faster and farther. If you haven't got ankle weights, try running in an old winter overcoat, in heavy leather boots, or with water-soaked towels tied around your legs.

At the same time that you work on your endurance you can also sharpen your ball skills. Why just run when you can run and practice your dribbling at the same time? Take your laps with a soccer ball, dribbling it before you at varying speeds. That way you build endurance and dribbling ability at the same time, killing two birds with one stone. Too, distance running is a lot more interesting when your mind is focused on the ball and on the perfection of your control rather than on the mere counting of laps.

Speed off the Mark

The most valuable kind of speed in soccer is speed generated in a fast burst off a turn or a standing position. Speed off the mark is what makes you a good defender or a good dribbler, and it is what brings you to a loose ball before your opponent. If you were not built long and lanky like a track star, that's OK. Your success in soccer depends on being able to cover only ten or twenty yards with lightning speed. You don't have to be able to beat everyone over the entire length of the field. You need quickness, flexibility, and agility—speed off the mark—and these qualities can be *developed*, through practice, by anyone.

Start out by covering the area between the goal and the eighteen-yard line. This distance of nearly twenty yards is already lined on your soccer field, and it provides a convenient space for developing quick speed. (Be sure you are warmed up—by running laps or doing calisthenics—before you try to work on bursts of speed. You're going to put a great strain on your body, and you ought not to shock it as well.) Start out by covering the eighteen yards as fast as you can. Count the number of steps that you take, and time yourself if you have a stopwatch.

The way you will build up speed off the mark is to train yourself to cover the same ground in fewer steps. It is the motion of the steps that takes all the time when you run. So practice stretching out your stride, taking fewer and fewer steps to cover the same ground. Work on pushing off with each foot as you run, not merely placing one foot in front of the other. As you learn to cover the same amount of ground with fewer steps you will see that your *times* will improve concurrently.

Once you have stretched out your stride and find that you are covering the eighteen yards much faster than before, you can begin to work on combining this new speed with the stop-and-go action that is so typical of game situations. Start your run facing into the goalmouth, then quickly whirl and run to the eighteen. There, instead of running past, try to stop on a dime, right on the line. Then whirl and run back toward the goal. Or you might vary this process by running one of these stretches backward. (In games you'll often be called upon to run backward, but few players practice this important skill.)

You can improve the "action" of your legs—

the speed with which you can actually get them to take successive steps—by running in place. Start out slowly, and then build up to the fastest speed you can manage. Remember to keep your knees out in front of you, as they would be if you were moving.

In games you will often have to recover from an off-balance position or get up off the ground and make a fast run. Such moments should be practiced too. Lie on the ground, and then jump up for your sprint. Perform a mock kick or head, and then run. Another common game situation is the need to break into a sharp sprint from a jog. Jog along the eighteen, then suddenly sprint in toward the goal. Jog out toward the midfield line, then turn and run into the goal. If you have cones (like the ones used to mark off a road when it's being repaired), set up a slalom course to simulate the presence of the opposing players who may often interfere with your fast run. You must be able to run, but you must also be able to *move as you run*.

Use your imagination to devise exercises that help develop speed off the mark. When you know what you are trying to achieve, self-generated exercises are often the most effective. Some players simply don't like the regimentation of "someone else's" exercises; others can generate better techniques for themselves because they are in touch with their own needs. Always try to make a game out of building yourself up, as opposed to creating so-called challenges which are often no more than exercises in masochism. You do have to work hard to improve, but you will invariably get the most benefit out of the time you spend in trying to improve if you spend it having *fun*.

Inner Speed

You cannot "will" yourself to be any faster than your natural endowments plus training will permit, but the mind does play a significant role in determining how fast you cover the distance between two points. Its role is partly involved in the alertness and awareness that are crucial for quick starts, and partly in your own feelings about how fast you are or can be. (If you think you are slow you can bet that you *will* be slow, slower at least than your top potential.)

Keep yourself focused at all times on the ball,

on your immediate opponents, on the location of your teammates, and on the general configuration of play. Speed off the mark that gets you to the ball first is often simply a matter of alertness—the fraction of a second that may be all you need to beat your opponent. And that fraction of a second can come from a quick mind as well as a quick pair of legs. If you are daydreaming, or hesitant, or afraid, all the physical training in the world will not get you to the ball on time.

Too, many players feel that they have a limited amount of speed, that they will never have any more, and that there is nothing they can do to increase it. But we *do* improve with training, and when that improvement occurs, we must *believe* in it. If you believe yourself to be slow you will drop off in a race for the ball. You will never reach your own limit because you do not give it a chance to show itself. This is especially critical with young players who may become faster as they grow older and stronger. Improvement can come at any time. It may be the result of physical growth or training, or it may come from a more relaxed attitude. Whatever the case, your own beliefs about your speed should not be overlooked as a factor. Don't "peg" yourself at a certain speed; just focus on where you're going, and pull out all the stops to get there. In running, especially over the short distances we are talking about, the idea of speed can well become the reality of speed. What is more important, though, is that if you believe within yourself that you will be beaten to the ball, you are likely to live out a self-fulfilling prophecy.

Overall Running Speed

This third aspect of running can only be improved through constant work. The techniques are the same as for endurance and speed off the mark. But to develop your overall running speed you should work on sprints of fifty to a hundred yards. Even a long run in soccer will rarely cover more than half the field.

SKILLS

As we have stressed over and over again in this book, the key to soccer is your ability to send and receive the ball in exactly the manner you desire. That ability does not come naturally (remember, soccer is the "unnatural sport")—it can only be gained through practice. Think of your body as a musical instrument. You cannot improvise and play good jazz (or classical, or rock!) until you know your notes and scales. You must master your instrument before real music comes out.

Fortunately, soccer is a game in which the skills can be practiced and learned in isolation, apart from the game situation. And the skills don't have to be "put together" before you can play. If you've mastered your ball control and defense completely, all of your skills will come together, will flow together, when the test, the match, arrives.

Two ways of practicing—juggling and the use of a wall—stand out above all the rest in their value to the soccer player (whatever his position), and we will deal with these two first.

Juggling

Juggling serves many purposes, but the most important is that it helps you develop a *feel for the ball*. An intimate relationship with the ball, a relationship of gentle mastery, is a primary requirement for any good soccer player. The ball must become a kind of extension of your body, something that you can move when you want to and where you want to. When you master the art of juggling, the smooth leather ball will begin to stick to you like a magnet.

Juggling is, quite simply, the ability to keep the ball in the air and to keep control of it, by yourself, for a long period of time.

Start by learning to keep the ball in the air with just your feet. Lift the ball up with your toe, then keep it in the air by tapping it gently on the underside with your instep. You will see that in order to retain control of the ball you have to stay on your toes all the time (to keep good position) and you have to learn to use a light touch. Be sure that your toe is pointed slightly upward, or the ball will fly away from you.

After you have learned to keep the ball bouncing on your feet, add your thighs to the game. Bounce the ball on the top of your thigh, keeping the thigh parallel to the ground. Then add your chest and head. When using your chest, you'll see that a great deal of cushioning is necessary. Head juggling requires a light touch too. Be sure to head the ball on your hairline, just as you would in a game, not on the crown of your head (that's tempting, since you're staying in one place).

The keys to successful juggling are concentration, staying on your toes for good position, and finding just the right touch for the ball to keep it in the air but close to you. These are all skills that you will use time and time again in actual game situations. You will also find that juggling itself is an effective technique in games—sometimes juggling is the *only* means by which you can take the ball around your opponent. But most of all, juggling gives you a feel for the ball. By juggling, you learn that you can make the ball do what you want, you learn just how hard or soft to touch it and still maintain control, you learn that you cannot control a ball without being on your toes and light on your feet.

And most important, this learning is not intellectual. Your *body* learns these things, your unconscious, your automatic muscular response system. You teach your bloodstream how to play, as it were. In a game, you no longer have to think about what you're doing. Your body *knows* what to do, because it's learned the touch, the feel, the skills, by heart.

Juggling is the fastest and best way to turn the unnatural movements that make up soccer into natural responses, reflexes. Psychologically, the player who knows that he can juggle knows that he is master of the ball And when the ball comes to him on the field, he is cool, always in command, never afraid that the difficulty of ball control will overcome him. That head set is precious indeed.

Using a Wall

Interestingly, team practice is perhaps the most inefficient way to learn and sharpen soccer skills. During scrimmages (practice games) each player handles the ball for only a few minutes—surely not enough time to perfect one's kicks, traps, dribbles, and defense. Even during team skills drills each player only touches the ball in rotation with the others on his team or in his group. What's important in soccer is that you be able to kick and trap in a game *perfectly* every time you're called upon to do so. To gain this perfection you need more intensive work than the formalistic, ritualistic kinds of group activity that characterize most team practices. You need to work on your own, practicing your kicks and traps over and over again. And then some more.

You have a friend who will help you practice. This friend does not talk to you, or encourage you, or compete with you. This friend always lets you do what you want, always lets you work on just what you want to work on. And he never wants to go home. He may be dull, but he's thoroughly helpful. He is a wall.

Playing against a wall is probably the best thing you can do to help yourself become a good soccer player. The effect is analogous to the aid that an automatic baseball pitcher can give to a batter trying to improve his hitting. You are able to kick to the wall time and time again without having to chase a ball or wait for a partner to return it to you. You are able to experience your accuracy and power on each kick and to make the necessary adjustments on the next kick. You can practice shots on goal, passes, long kicks, increasing the distance of your throw-ins, trapping high or low balls—any of the kicking or receiving skills in soccer.

Concentrate on the ball and on how you kick or trap. If you have problems, try to stop and analyze what's wrong. Work carefully and in a relaxed manner to bring your skills to perfection. The great advantage of the wall is that it gives you rapid-fire practice without any pressure to perform. There's no one watching you, or waiting for you, or depending on you for a play. So work at your own speed, as fast or as slowly as you like. The wall gives you your own time to practice in private. If you work against a wall regularly you will see your game improve immeasurably.

Specific Skills and Group Work

Every skill in soccer can be practiced in drill form, and many of the drills, the exercises, are suitable for use with the whole team or with smaller groups. There are a great number of such exercises—new ones are constantly being created by inventive coaches and players (you

can create your own too!)—and any attempt to list them all would fill a book by itself. In the following pages we will review some of the classic exercises, mainly those oriented toward developing skills already discussed in this book.

Dribbling

Safety cones (of the sort, already mentioned, used to mark off a roadway that's being worked on or painted) are most useful for exercises in dribbling as well as in the development of other skills. The most familiar dribbling exercise with cones is to set up a group of them in a slalom course, each cone ten to fifteen feet apart. The cones needn't be in a straight line—in fact it's better if they're somewhat staggered. The idea, of course, is to dribble around all the cones as fast and with as much control as possible. You can also use cones for a one-on-one drill. Here the player with the ball stands behind a cone, with his opponent on the other side of it. The dribbler tries to dribble past both cone and opponent. The cone serves as a kind of blocking interference, but it also functions as an obstacle.

Group dribbling requires lots of concentration and is a good trainer. Each player on the team dribbles with his own ball within a circumscribed area (such as the penalty area or the center circle). Every player must dribble continuously, maintaining control of his own ball and avoiding the balls of the other players. This drill really forces you to keep your dribble close. To add extra spice and really separate out the most alert players, change the rules so that each player *tries* to knock each other ball out of the circle while still maintaining control over his own ball. The last player left is, of course, the winner.

Dribbling exercises don't have to be complex or structured too heavily. Having a defender and a dribbler, or two defenders and a dribbler, constantly work against each other is a perfectly adequate form of gaining dribbling expertise. In general, you should try to dribble as much as possible in order to develop the intimate relationship with the ball mentioned earlier. When running laps, always take a ball along so that you can dribble at the same time. A little dribbling practice every day, even in the backyard, will go a long way.

Heading

You can practice heading against a wall or with a partner, and by juggling on your head. But these methods miss an important aspect of heading—dealing with a challenging opponent. Try to practice heading in a threesome. Have one player stand in front of you, and have the third member of your group throw the ball for a head. This way you learn to jump up to head with an "opponent" in front of you. If you don't jump, the ball will merely bounce into the "obstacle" player. When you feel confident, have the obstacle player *compete* with you for the head. You must learn to go up for a head when challenged, without fear.

Cones are also useful in heading practice. Set up a cone five feet in front of you. Then jump forward for your head, landing on the other side of the cone. Using a person in front helps you learn to go *up* for a head; using a cone helps you learn to go *forward*. Both directions are important for good heading.

Still another useful technique is to connect a ball to a rope that is tied to a tree limb or some other high crossbar. Send the ball swinging in different directions, and meet it with solid headers.

Work in small groups, using at least one person as a passing outlet. Practice heading the ball *down* to your pass receiver's feet. High balls are difficult to control. Learn to bring the ball back under control from a head play.

Practice heading from a prone position. Lying on your stomach, have your partner throw the ball so that you can head it. Rise up off the ground *without lifting yourself on your arms,* and head the ball back to him. This exercise is excellent for learning to head low balls, and it is also a terrific conditioner for the back, neck, thighs, and stomach.

Kicking and Trapping

Kicking and trapping can be learned on your own with the help of a wall, and are perhaps *best* learned in this way. But don't merely try to blast the ball against the wall and then trap it. Practice all the different kinds of kicks—instep, side of the foot, volley, and so on—and practice them with varying degrees of force. The variety

of pace you will need in a game is infinite, so work on everything from a little pat to a downfield boot. At the same time, you should be honing your accuracy. Pick spots on the wall, and really try to place your kicks right on them. Practice kicking while standing and while moving as well. Practice kicking off balance—sometimes you'll have to kick that way in a game. In fact, try to imagine every possible kicking situation in a game and work on it. That's what practicing is all about. It's far better to make your mistakes against a blank wall than against an opponent in a match.

Trapping practice against a wall should go beyond just controlling the kicks you make as they come back to you. Make your kicks so that you can practice different kinds of traps too. If you have trouble kicking to create a specific kind of trapping situation—such as a high dropping ball—just throw the ball against the wall to make it happen. Practice one-touch play as well. Kick the ball against the wall, trap the rebound, and learn to kick again (and accurately!) before the ball has a chance to drop to the ground.

Trapping practice against a wall lacks one important feature that you cannot do without, so it's not enough. Just as in heading, you need to learn to perform your trapping skills under pressure and in concert with the other members of your team. A wonderful ability to trap and control a ball means nothing if that ability falls apart when you are challenged or when you have little room in which to work.

Practice kicking and receiving in groups of four. Two players start out as the kickers and receivers. The other two are defenders. At first, the defenders should play loosely and without too much vigor. The kickers and receivers play the ball back and forth to each other. Gradually, the defenders should make an increasing effort to interfere with the kicks and traps. The area in which both contesting players can move should be limited to a relatively small circle so that this is not a passing drill but an exercise in basic ball sending and control.

Passing

Passing is best practiced in small groups, since if this is done, you are always passing *to* someone, and are usually trying to avoid someone else at the same time. But you can practice passing on your own, with a wall. This is a convenient way to practice, coincidentally enough, the wall pass.

Set up a target on the wall, and practice passing to this target until you can hit it at will from a variety of angles and with a variety of kicking styles. Then begin to kick the ball at an angle so that it will rebound away from where you are standing. Run to receive the ball at the spot at which you have calculated it should arrive, a give-and-go play with the wall as your teammate. You should be making a triangle, with the wall as its apex. Do this over and over, until you can hit your spot from any angle and retrieve the rebounded "pass."

The standard way of practicing passing, though, is in small group work. The typical method of standing in a circle and passing the ball back and forth or around the circle is really not very useful. You should set up situations in which you are under pressure and you have to move. Playing small-scale games (two-on-two, two-on-three, and so on) is the most helpful method. If this is done with four players, two passing players should move constantly to create space around two defenders who are trying hard to intercept the play. Start by focusing on wall and lateral passes, and progress to through passes. Remember that each time you pass you must then move into an open space for the return pass. When you "give," you then have to "go." Make the game even harder by setting up a rule that the passers are not allowed to dribble. This game is also an excellent way to build endurance.

The through pass should be mastered perfectly, for it is the most potent weapon available to an offense for setting up goals. Play with three offensive players against two defenders (the defenders can have a third player who acts as goalkeeper). One offensive player has the ball, while the other two are guarded by the two defenders. All three offensive players must move around and work hard to free up a space for the penetrating pass. The player with the ball must then pass through the defenders to his breaking teammate. If the pass is too hard it will go past the receiver and be fielded by the goalkeeper. If it is too soft, the receiver will have to wait or come back for it, and the play will probably be broken up by a defender. After each pass is executed, whether successful or not, the players should return to the starting point and begin again. Practice is the *only* way to gain a sense of what's required for effective through passing, and all offensive players should work very hard on this. Without good penetration ability any team must rely on luck alone for its goals.

Tackling

A good way to learn the art of tackling is to begin by tackling the ball rather than a player *with* the ball. This is a necessary skill in its own right, and it provides an opportunity to learn concentration on the all-important ball, rather than on an opponent's legs.

Set up two cones about twenty yards apart. The tackler should stand midway between the cones. His partner then rolls or passes the ball to the outside of one cone (the partner stands about twenty yards in front of the tackler), and the tackler runs to the ball, sliding for a tackle and sending the ball away. He quickly returns to his original, midway position, and his partner passes to the outside of the other cone. The tackler must then tackle that ball away too, and quickly return to the center again.

The tackling of the player with the ball should be done in small groups to approximate match conditions. Try using only two defenders against three offensive players. This means that there is always a theoretical extra player for a passing outlet. The defenders cannot simply rush in for a tackle, then, for they are outnumbered. They must press in on the passers and create an opportunity by forcing a pass or anticipating one and coming in for the tackle only when it is safe and properly timed. Outnumbering the defenders compels this need for precise and accurate timing, and timing is what makes the difference in tackling.

Creating Exercises That Work

There are so many plays in soccer, so many subtle differences in each situation, that it would be futile to list all of the possible drills. As an individual or as part of a team, though, you should concentrate on your weaknesses, concentrate on what you *don't* know. All too often athletes have a tendency to go through a mechanical and self-congratulatory routine of demonstrating their already accomplished skills. Go the other way. Work on what's hard for you.

And work on what's critical. Work on corner kicks, on through passes, on being able to move the ball downfield with a series of wall passes, on learning to get back on defense and to support your teammates by moving into open spaces. Work on fundamentals that are always being combined and recombined to create the fluid play of soccer. Don't feel that you are ignorant of a specific way to practice any given skill or play. Make one up! There's certainly no rule that says you can't apply your own imagination and ingenuity to improving your own or your team's game. In fact, the great teams of our era have become great because of their creativity—because they had the vision and the guts to try something new. Never think of soccer as merely a game of the body. It is a game of the mind as well. Just as you should always maintain an analytic mind regarding strategies and tactics, you should also focus your brain on how to improve the component *parts* of your game. Improvise. See what works. Don't be afraid to try new things, and don't be afraid to fail. There's no magic key to success. You have to work at your game, and you have to think it through. Break down your game in your mind. Then build it up again on the practice field.

TIPS FROM THE STARS: ADVICE TO A YOUNG PLAYER

One of the many things I learned while on the bench was that a substitute must prepare himself for the game in the same way he would if he were a starter. Even though I knew I was not going to start, I still prepared myself—doing warm-ups, ball control skills—just as I always did before a game. Then, if I was called upon, even in the last ten minutes, I would be ready. . . . Personal pride is involved in starting one game and sitting out the next. You don't like the implication that someone is better than you are. But I go back again to my whole philosophy of winning and ask myself, "Am I playing as well as I can?" If the answer is yes to that question and I am still taken out of the game, then I am not so concerned, because my own standards have been met. I think as long as a player can take that attitude he's come out a winner no matter where or how much he plays.

Kyle Rote, Jr., Beyond the Goal

I was dedicated in myself. In my younger years, when I was 12 to 17 years of age, I was my own trainer. I used to go out in the mornings and work for a couple of hours. That was every day. And I think this has stood by me in these years. It has helped me tremendously. I always remember that period of time when I worked so hard. And I think this is where I got my ability that has led to later successes.

Jimmy Johnstone, in Soccer World

11 Equipment

Soccer requires very little equipment and is among the least expensive of team sports. Because you do not need very much equipment you should be careful in your selection and purchase the highest quality possible. Soccer equipment does not wear out quickly, and even shoes—the hardest-used item—will last many years if they are well made.

If you are not using a uniform, any T-shirt will do. Be sure that your T-shirt is not too tight. Your movements should be unrestricted, and you should be able to breathe easily. Soccer uniforms can be obtained from most sporting goods stores. Be sure that your uniforms were designed with soccer in mind. You'll need two different shirts—a light one for warm-weather play and a heavier one to keep your body warm during cold seasons. Numbers are quite irrelevant in this age of "total football" (see Chapter 8, "Alignments and Tactics"), though the goalie usually wears number 1.

Your shorts must fit loosely. They should never hamper the movement of your legs. Baggy shorts are fine—just be sure that they have a good drawstring to hold them up. A player with his shorts down around his ankles can psych out the other team, but he'll have trouble running very fast.

Shoes are the key piece of soccer equipment, as is fitting for a game played with the feet. Be sure that your soccer shoes are of the best possible quality—trying to save a few dollars on their cost can be penny-wise and pound-foolish. It is critical that the shoes fit properly. They should be made of soft leather, and the fit should be quite snug. Most experts say that the shoe should "fit like a glove." You must bear in mind that shoes, being leather, will probably stretch a bit during wear—players often wear soccer shoes that are a half size smaller than their street shoes. Soccer shoes can also be molded to fit your feet when you first get them. To do this, lace the shoes on your feet and soak them in a tub of lukewarm water for a quarter of an hour. Then go outside and walk or run in them for another half hour. Water makes the leather tighten, and it will tighten in such a way as to fit the specific contour of your foot exactly. During the season you should use saddle soap on the shoes to keep them soft, and polish to keep them looking good.

Most players will have only one pair or style of shoes, but several styles are available, and you should have a selection if possible. There is a flat-soled type, similar to a tennis or deck shoe, which is used on astroturf or frozen surfaces when ordinary studs do not give good traction. But these shoes are rarely used. There are also studded shoes with only six nylon studs on the sole which are used for muddy conditions. The studs can be screwed in and out with a wrench, and changed to suit the field conditions. These studs, fewer in number and more penetrating than the studs of a conventional shoe, do not clog up with mud as badly and will give extra traction on a sloppy field. The conventional shoe today has a sole of molded rubber with fourteen permanent small studs. This shoe gives the best traction on a wide variety of playing surfaces, and if you have only one pair of soccer shoes, this is the style you should use. High quality is far more important than any manufacturer's label. Look for a good fit between the sole and the leather uppers—a tearing away of the sole is the most common problem of poor quality shoes. This ruins the shoe, and it can also be dangerous if it happens when you are running at high speed.

Your socks may be high or low—it all depends on the kind of outfitting your team decides to use. High socks are, of course, preferable if you are going to use shin guards, and they have a sharper, more classic soccer look on the field. If you do use high socks, make sure that your means of holding them up, whether it be elastic, string, cloth, or tape, is not so tight that it cuts off circulation.

Shin pads are in disfavor now, for they make it more difficult for the player to run and maneuver. However, they are useful for younger players who have not yet learned to keep from hacking their opponents when going for the ball, and for players whose shins are injury-prone. In general, though, the less extra equipment you are carrying around with you, the better.

Knee pads, however, weigh very little, do not impede your ability to run or turn or kick, and can provide a real physical and psychological advantage. They provide definite protection for the knees, and if you wear them you will probably feel freer to go in for sliding tackles. Knee pads can also give you a slight extra control when you are trapping.

Teams and individuals should get the best quality leather balls available. Like good soccer shoes, a good soccer ball will last for many years, whereas a poor quality ball can actually present physical dangers. A cheap ball that soaks up water on a wet field, for example, rather than shedding water as a good ball will, can become heavy and cause foot injuries when kicked.

The ball should be a number five leather ball, twenty-seven inches in diameter and constructed of thirty-two hand-stitched panels. The ball should weigh sixteen ounces fully inflated. (Youngsters under twelve might look for a number four ball, which is slightly lighter.) Be sure to follow the manufacturer's instructions for inflating the ball. A ball that is too fully packed with air or contains too little air is not a soccer ball. It is something that might have been a soccer ball if it had been properly inflated. A ball that is too soft performs improperly. A ball that is too hard or too heavy can cause injuries to the kicker. Be sure that your ball has good quality stitching so that it will keep its shape, and also be sure that the leather is waterproofed so that you don't wind up kicking something that has become rocklike during wet weather. The ball should be kept clean and treated with saddle soap and silicone waterproofing regularly.

Goalies need special equipment. Goalies should wear elbow pads and knee pads so that they can dive for balls without fear of injuring themselves. Some goalies wear gloves all the time to get a better grip on the ball, but all goalies should always wear gloves when the field is wet. A wet ball is terribly difficult to hold onto—a goalie who does not wear gloves when there is moisture on the field is simply asking for trouble. Gloves are also extremely important to the goalie during cold weather, when the fingers just don't work as well. A goalie also needs a shirt that is different in color from those worn by his teammates (this is a law of the game). And on very sunny days the goalie should avail himself of that simplest of solutions—a hat.

No team should take the field without having an emergency first-aid kit on the bench. There should be smelling salts, absorbent cotton, bandaging apparatus, ace bandages, ankle braces (ace bandages that look something like socks), antiseptic ointments, knee and elbow pads, small splints, chemical ice, heat packs, and so on. Soccer is not the roughest of games, but you should always be prepared for minor injuries. You should always know where the nearest doctor or hospital is, in case anything serious happens.

There is one piece of extra equipment which few teams pack, but it is one of the most important items in any list of necessary supplies. *Extra shoelaces!*

12
Care of
Minor Injuries

VOCABULARY

1. *Ligament:* A band of fibrous tissue that crosses a joint and holds adjacent bones in place.
2. *Sprain:* A pulled ligament.
3. *Tendon:* The end of a muscle which attaches to a bone.
4. *Strain:* A pulled muscle or tendon.
5. *Contusion:* A bruised muscle, tendon, or ligament.
6. *Fracture:* Any break in the continuity of a bone—may range from a slight crack to a complete crush with soft tissue damage.
7. *Dislocation:* Occurs when bones which form a joint slip away from each other beyond their normal positions and is usually accompanied by torn ligaments.

The information in this chapter was supplied by Dr. Steven H. Sewall, specialist in orthopedics, Sudbury, Massachusetts.

It is often very difficult to determine on the field whether the injured player is suffering from a strain, a sprain, a contusion, a fracture, or a dislocation. All of these injuries cause pain, swelling, tenderness, loss of motion, deformity, and discoloration (reddish, *not* black and blue, at least initially). Indeed, due to swelling a sprained ankle may sometimes appear to be more deformed than a fractured ankle.

A player who has these symptoms (pain, swelling, tenderness, loss of motion, deformity, discoloration) should *not* be allowed to continue playing. Because injuries can easily be made worse, the rule for all soccer players must be, "If in doubt, sit it out." You have only one body, and it must be cared for lovingly. The so-called bravery of playing when in severe pain is really bravado, and bravado is ultimately destructive to both the player and the team.

Severe *pain, tenderness,* and *loss of motion* are associated with the most serious injuries—strains, sprains, contusions, fractures, and dislocations—so one should never try to "fight the pain" and continue playing. The most serious deformities, with angulation and unnatural positioning of body parts and lengthening or shortening of extremities, occur with dislocations and fractures. If there is a fracture, the player may also experience *grating* sensations called *crepitation*.

When there's an injury on the field, and no trainer or doctor is available, one always hears a great debate about whether to apply cold or heat to the injury. There is nothing to debate. When the injury is associated with bones, ligaments, or tendons, emergency treatment *never* involves the application of heat. In all cases of sprains, strains, and minor contusions, you should apply *cold*. *Ice packs* and *compression* (pressure) should be applied to relieve and prevent swelling and to provide support. Heat can actually increase swelling and pain and aggravate the injury.

All bad injuries, such as fractures and dislocations (and serious strains, sprains, or contusions), should be *"splinted as they lay,"* immobilizing the joint above and below the area of injury. Splinting should be done no matter how short the travel time to a doctor or a hospital may be. Splinting will relieve pain; stave off further injury to the muscles, nerves, and blood vessels; and prevent simple fractures from becoming compound (more complicated and serious).

Never try to straighten a deformed bone or joint on the field. This job *must* be left to a trained physician. Too, if the bone is sticking out through the skin, you should try to control the bleeding with a sterile (if possible) pressure dressing before applying the splint. Be extremely careful not to let the exposed bone slip back beneath the skin, as this will "seed" the area with dirt and increase the likelihood of infection.

Muscle problems are perhaps less serious than those of the bones or ligaments, but they can be just as disabling. A pulled muscle (the common name for a muscle strain) or a traumatized muscle will be painful, tight, and possibly swollen. The general rule of thumb is that *pain* should take a player out of the game. If you are suffering from light pain you can continue playing. But if your pain is in any way out of the ordinary, there is no heroism in going on—you should then come out. For not only can continued activity on a severely strained or bruised

muscle make the condition worse, but you may also be suffering from a fracture that only *feels* like a strained or bruised muscle.

The initial treatment for pulled or bruised muscles is the same as that for bone and ligament injuries. The first goal is to reduce swelling, so the first treatment is the application of *cold* (an ice pack) to the injured area. Cold is the proper treatment for at least the first twenty-four hours, and as we shall see, cold may be the appropriate treatment long after that. You should also apply compression to a muscle injury—via an ace bandage or by pressing your hand on the ice pack or dressing. This too helps reduce swelling.

A player with a muscle injury on the field is often told to "walk it off." *This is very poor advice.* You should never "walk off" an injury— you should *get* off it. Walking on an injury could increase the damage.

Bleeding is another medical area that is often misunderstood by the lay person. If there is heavy bleeding, with the blood pumping and gushing out (from a cut in a major leg artery, for example), you should immediately apply direct pressure to the lacerated area. Most important, you should **not** apply a tourniquet. Tourniquets definitely cause more damage than they are worth, and they're the worst way to treat heavy bleeding. They cut off all circulation to the wounded area (which is certainly *not* desirable), and they can even cause gangrene. The *right* way to stop heavy bleeding is to apply pressure dressings. *Pressing,* not *wrapping,* is the proper approach. If no medical dressings are available, you might take a shirt, for example, and *press it hard directly on the wound.*

When bleeding is not severe, it is all right to keep on playing, but you must bear in mind that the motion of the leg as you run, opening and closing the cut, will make the bleeding worse. If possible, you should cover the bleeding area with a pressure dressing. Sutures (stitches) can wait until the game is over, as long as the bleeding is not too bad (you have to be the judge of this). You can wait until after the game, but you should *not* wait until the next day. Open wounds should not be left unattended for more than five or six hours—or you're likely to develop an infection. Be sure that the wound is cleaned and sutured (if necessary) within this time.

Toe pain may or may not indicate a fracture, and there is no way to tell without an X ray. You may still continue to play with toe pain, even if the toe is in fact broken, since little treatment is available anyway. Ordinarily the broken toe is taped or splinted to a toe next to it—if you think that you may have a toe fracture you ought to tape up the injured toe in this way until you can get to a doctor.

If you experience swelling and pain on the top of your foot near the beginning of the toes, you may have what is called a "stress fracture." This is a hairline fracture of the metatarsal bones, and the fracture will often not show up in an X ray until a week or more after the injury has occurred. Stress fractures result, as their name implies, from an overstressing of bones which are too thin to tolerate hard running. Stress fractures are usually experienced by people who are out of condition and begin to run too hard on undeveloped bones. As you get in better shape, the bones thicken and the risk of a stress fracture becomes minimal. But if you should have pain and swelling for more than a week in the area where your shoelaces end, go to a doctor for an X ray and further treatment.

Head injuries are not always serious, but we should always be extremely careful about observing symptoms after head injuries occur. Of course, the obvious rule is to stop playing as long as you are experiencing pain or abnormal feelings in your head. A *concussion* is a momentary loss of consciousness, a loss of memory of the accident, and it is usually accompanied by disorientation. There are many degrees of concussion—some concussions are very trivial; others are as serious as an accident can be. The distinction is usually found in the number and the quality of the initial symptoms and in the persistence of symptoms. In most cases a concussion simply "goes away." Essentially what happens is that the head gets traumatized and that there is a slight swelling of the brain. There is often difficulty in identifying one's name, location, date of birth, and so on—a kind of temporary amnesia sets in. Additional and subsequent symptoms include nausea, vomiting, lack of ability to move the extremities, poor reflexes, unequal size of pupils, dizziness, high blood pressure, severe headaches, and blurred or double vision. *If you experience head contact in a game, and you have any of these symptoms, either immediately after the head contact or later, see a doctor right away.*

One should not become terrorized by a head injury or the prospect of one—only a tiny fraction of head injuries are serious. You should observe yourself closely, though, for a serious head injury is indeed a serious matter.

On the field, be very careful about *moving* a player with a head injury, for such injuries are often complicated by neck injuries. If you move a person with an injured neck, the risk of worsening his condition is very great. The general treatment for concussion is complete rest, and the symptoms will usually subside. If you haven't lost consciousness you do not have a *concussion*. But be aware of the symptoms listed above so that you will know when you must get to a doctor quickly.

TREATMENT AFTER THE INJURY AND PERIODS OF RECOVERY

As we have said, in *every* case the first treatment is **cold** and **pressure**. This reduces swelling (which is the body's response to trauma) and speeds the healing process. Cold compresses or cold soaks should continue for at least twenty-four hours.

The initial cooling should help reduce the swelling appreciably. Naturally, the course of treatment must always depend on the severity of the injury, so any "rules" for treatment must necessarily be general—to be applied thoughtfully to each individual case. After the first twenty-four hours (this applies to all of the injuries discussed except bleeding), you may begin to apply **heat** to the injury. That heat must always be **wet heat**—hot towels, hot baths (soaks), or hydroculators which are made for this purpose and are available in most drugstores. Hot water bottles and electric heating pads are *not* really very effective for the treatment of injuries.

As we've said, the rules are general. The application of wet heat is the next stage of treatment, *but only if the heat does not increase the swelling.* You must watch out for this. Sometimes, if the wet heat is applied too early, it will simply cause the injury to swell up again. In that case, stop applying the wet heat immediately and go back to cold. Another acceptable method of treatment after the first twenty-four hours is *contrasting baths,* the alternating application of wet heat and cold. This method is fine, but again, if the swelling increases, stay with cold.

Aside from and along with the application of cold and heat, the best treatment is complete rest. One of the best ways to turn an ordinary injury into a *chronic condition* is to go out and start playing again before you are ready. Until that time you should get as much rest as you can, walking with crutches if you like and keeping your injured area elevated as much as possible. When you do begin to use the injured part again, don't go wild with it. Work back into full activity slowly, letting the weakened part gradually build up its strength. You have only one body—it's not worth risking a lifetime disability just to get back on the field a week or a few days sooner.

But when are you ready to return to play? Obviously, you are not ready until you are *fully healed.* Anything less is simply asking for trouble and complications. One would always rather play than not play, but you have to resist the temptation. The criteria for complete healing are as follows:
1. No pain on motion.
2. Full range of motion.
3. No tenderness.
4. No redness or black and blue.
5. No increased heat in the injured area.
6. Return of normal strength.

In the course of healing, muscles will sometimes *atrophy,* or become smaller than they were originally. This process may continue even after the disappearance of all other symptoms. Atrophy is not really serious, and you may return to play even with atrophied muscles as long as all of the criteria for complete healing have been met. A lightly bruised muscle may put you out of action for a week or two. If you suffer more serious injuries, such as pulled ligaments, dislocations, and so on, it will often be at least six weeks before you are back to normal, and you should not try to push that schedule. Your body needs time, and it does not care whether you are impatient or not. If you are unlucky enough to sustain a fracture, which is fairly rare in soccer, you may be on the sidelines for as much as a year.

No one but a doctor is really qualified to diagnose a soccer injury. Different kinds of injury, such as damage to cartilage or the ligaments, may well require *surgical repair* and often cannot heal at all without surgery. For this reason, no player should simply hobble around and wait for his injury to "get better." In many instances the injury will *not* get better without proper diagnosis and treatment. Too, in certain cases the longer you wait for treatment, the more serious the injury can become.

So get proper treatment right away. If you don't you may never play soccer again. To avoid a doctor because of the time or expense involved is perhaps the most penny-wise and pound-foolish act imaginable.

When you return to play, don't forget to take it easy on yourself. After your body has been repaired or has repaired itself, it takes considerable time for it to heal fully, even if all of the symptoms are gone. Exercise only moderately; allow yourself plenty of rest; and be closely tuned in to *any* sensations you feel in the area of your injury. Pain and other sensations are your body's way of telling you "something's happening here," and you shouldn't ignore symptoms merely because you want to play.

13
For Further Reading in Soccer

Al Miller, *Winning Soccer* (Henry Regnery).

Paul Gardner, *The Simplest Game* (Little, Brown).

Paul Gardner and Phil Woosnam, *Sports Illustrated Soccer* (J. B. Lippincott).

Paul Gardner, *Pele: The Master and His Method*.

Ken Jones and Pat Welton, *Soccer Skills and Tactics* (Crown).

Enzo Domini, *The Book of Soccer* (Little, Brown).

Paul E. Harris, *Goal!* (Soccer for Americans).

Chuck Cascio, *Soccer U.S.A.* (Robert B. Luce, Inc.).

Brian Glanville, *Goalkeepers Are Crazy* (available from Mr. Soccer, Dallas, Texas).

Martin Tyler, ed., *The Sportsman's World of Soccer* (Marshall Cavendish).

The Sixty Memorable Matches (Marshall Cavendish).

Football's All-Time Greats (Marshall Cavendish).

Paul and Larry Harris, *Fair or Foul?* (Soccer for Americans).

Gunter Lammich and Heinz Kadow, *Warm Up for Soccer* (Sterling Publishing Co.).

George Best, *On the Ball*.

Brian Glanville, *The History of the World Cup*.

Zander Hollander, ed., *The Complete Handbook of Soccer* (annual) (Signet).

Kyle Rote, Jr., *Beyond the Goal* (Berkley).

John Arlott, *Soccer: The Great Ones* (Pelham).

Nobby Stiles, *Soccer, My Battlefield* (S. Paul).

Kenneth Wheeler, *Champions of Soccer* (Pelham).

C. Alcock, *Football: The Association Games* (G. Bell & Sons, published in 1928).

John Allen, *Soccer for Americans* (Grosset & Dunlap).

James Alan, *Ball of Fire* (Pelham).

Danny Blanchflower, *Soccer Book* (F. Muller).

Peter Bonetti, *Leaping to Fame* (S. Paul).

Ralph Leslie Finn, *World Cup, 1970* (R. Hale).

Maurice Galsworthy, *The Encyclopedia of Association Football* (R. Hale).

Denis Howell, *Soccer Refereeing* (Pelham).

Basil G. Kane, *Soccer for American Spectators* (A. S. Barnes).

Bobby Moore, *England! England!* (S. Paul).

Allen Wade, *Soccer: Guide to Training and Coaching* (Funk and Wagnalls).

Most of the publishers whose names you find unfamiliar are English publishers. Your library may carry these books, or your local bookseller can order them.

Index